PRODUCT MASTERY

PRODUCT MASTERY

A MASTERCLASS IN PRODUCT MANAGEMENT

ABHISHEK AGARWAL

Visit my website at www.bookshopclub.com

First Printing: Dec 2023

ISBN: 979-8-8689-9918-5

PRAISE FOR AUTHOR

"Abhishek has created a comprehensive primer for anyone interested in embarking on the career journey to mastering Product Management. His chapter on AI ML in Product Management is clearly explained in practical, non-technical terms. He lays out a thorough framework including providing easy-to-understand definitions, logical steps and necessary context to guide the reader through an expertly distilled guide to the key considerations of managing the complex landscape of using AI ML in product management and developing a commanding grasp of AI ML product management, and all the integration that entails. It is a must-read for any product manager." - Dr. Deborah Wall, PhD, MPhil, MBA

"This insightful chapter illuminates the emerging world of AI product management. The author provides a meticulous overview of core AI/ML concepts and introduces practical frameworks like AIM-PLUS to guide organizations through progressive AI adoption phases. He astutely emphasizes building multidisciplinary teams of data scientists, ML engineers, and domain experts as a keystone for AI success. Crucial topics including data acquisition, model operations, transparency, and continuous enhancement are covered comprehensively, elucidating real-world applications. Insightful case studies of AI integration at Netflix and Uber demonstrate how these technologies, when strategically applied, can profoundly transform user experiences and entire industries. The chapter concludes by underscoring the widening divide between visionary AI-first companies and legacy organizations lagging in adoption. Overall, this well-structured chapter serves as an essential guide for product managers and executives seeking to harness AI's power ethically in their offerings. It delivers invaluable guidance to organizations aiming to gain a competitive edge by embracing AI." – Sridhar Vishnubhotla, MS, MBA, Head of innovation.

DEDICATION

To the Dreamers who embrace technology's potential,
This dedication is a tribute to your resilience and unyielding belief
in technology's power. Like your own journey, let these pages
remind you that innovation and technology together propel us
towards progress. With humility, remember that achievements
spring from a blend of human ingenuity and tech's capabilities.

As you march forward, may these words inspire you to seize
technology's potential, and transform your dreams into reality with
humility and gratitude.

With admiration

CONTENTS

FOREWORD i

PREFACE iii

1 Introduction to Product Management 1

2 Product Strategy 8

3 Know your Customers 22

4 Priotizations 39

5 Implementations 68

6 Communications 101

7 Building Teams 118

8 Innovation Culture 147

9 AI/ML Product Management 164

10 Author Note 193

ABOUT THE AUTHOR 195

FOREWORD

What is in common between all these software products: Amazon's recommendation engine, Spotify's music suggestions, Tesla's autopilot evolution, Netflix content recommendations, Google RankBrain, and Airbnb's dynamic pricing? I bet you have the answer already – the power of AI. This power gave a new meaning to the role of a product manager.

A decade ago, the perception of product management was quite different. It was often seen as a more narrowly defined role, primarily focused on ensuring a product met the specified requirements and deadlines. In recent years, the landscape of product management has undergone a significant transformation. First, with the concept of customer-centricity, which shifted focus from building features to solving customer problems. Second, lean startup and other experimentation frameworks allow product managers to accurately forecast the success of products before they are built. Add to it cross-functional collaboration and focus on user experience. But this was just the beginning.

The world of product management is now rapidly evolving, especially with the advent of AI and ML. AI and ML have become integral to product management, shaping industries and creating groundbreaking products that enhance user experiences, save costs, and drive innovation.

Abhishek Agarwal's innovative book extends the discussion of product management from feature prioritization and implementation to a heightened emphasis on data-driven decision-making, regulatory compliance, and ethical considerations, particularly in the context of generative AI. Starting from basics in an engaging and educational way, Abhishek takes his readers step-by-step into realms of complex platform solutions, continuous evaluation, and AI- powered product solutions across industries.

There is a dire need for such a book. While there are multiple books available on the product management discipline, this book provides the end-to-end journey into modern product management, starting from basic definitions and foundational concepts into the complex implementation of AI and ML. Relevant exercises and case studies make this journey palpable and real.

This book reflects Abhishek's expertise in technology and product management and his commitment to knowledge sharing. I had the pleasure of working with Abhishek at Amazon Web Services (AWS). His work at AWS, particularly in SageMaker products, showcases his visionary approach and strategic insights.

The book demystifies the complexities of product management, offering valuable insights and strategies for professionals, entrepreneurs, and students. Abhishek's work goes beyond technological advancement; he places a significant emphasis on ethical considerations in AI and machine learning.

I wouldn't want to hold you any longer. You are up to a treat. This book's content has the potential to reshape industries, inspire minds, and guide individuals in the ever-evolving landscape of product management and technology. Hope you enjoy the journey!

Mariya Breyter, Ph.D., Author of Agile Product and Project
MANAGEMENT, APRESS, 2022
Marlboro, NJ. OCTOBER 2023

PREFACE

Creating this book has been a significant undertaking, reflecting my personal experiences, challenges, and growth in the fields of product management and business. As I sit down to write this preface, memories of numerous discussions, collaborations, and insights flood my mind, shaping the way I see the world. This book is the result of those experiences, a compilation of insights from innovation, strategy, leadership, and a steadfast commitment to excellence.

My upbringing in rural India as a first-generation college student was marked by both obstacles and aspirations. Each setback I encountered, each triumph I celebrated, has left a mark on my trajectory. From the Indian Institute of Technology (IIT) to Yale University, I embarked on a transformative path that propelled me from modest beginnings to the forefront of product management.

The driving force behind this book is to serve as a guide for those navigating the landscape of product management and business. I'm aware of the challenges confronted by first-generation students, individuals from diverse backgrounds, and those aspiring to bridge the gap between theory and practice. This book is intended to demystify the complexities of product management and present insights, strategies, and narratives that resonate universally.

Drawing from my tenure at Amazon Web Services (AWS), where I spearheaded the development of SageMaker products, I aim to impart lessons learned, best practices, and transformative methodologies for product development. From the inception of ideas to the culmination of launches, this book offers a comprehensive guide that blends theory with tangible insights from the real world.

The world of product management is rapidly evolving, especially with the advent of AI and machine learning. These technologies are extending access to cutting-edge solutions and reshaping the way we approach innovation. However, this transformation also necessitates a heightened emphasis on ethical considerations, particularly in the context of generative AI. As AI becomes more integral to our lives, product managers play a crucial role in ensuring that technology is developed and deployed ethically and responsibly.

My aspiration for this book transcends mere instructional value. I hope it becomes a wellspring of inspiration, a repository of ideas, and a compass for those aspiring to leave an indelible mark in the realm of product management and business. Whether you're a seasoned professional, an aspiring entrepreneur, or an inquisitive student, my aim is to equip you with the tools, frameworks, and wisdom required to navigate the ever-evolving landscape of innovation and strategy.

As you immerse yourself in the pages of this book, my earnest wish is that you not only discover invaluable insights but also find a reflection of your own aspirations and experiences. Product management is a fusion of artistry and science, a domain where a blend of creativity and strategy shapes the contours of the future. I invite you to accompany me on this exploration, a path of discovery, revelation, and growth—a path that has the potential to reshape industries and influence minds.

With utmost anticipation,
Abhishek K Agarwal

ACKNOWLEDGMENTS

In the process of creating this book on product management, I extend my heartfelt gratitude to all who contributed. To my editors, collaborators, reviewers, colleagues, friends, and family, your support and insights have been invaluable.

To my wife, Ruhi, your unwavering support and inspiration have been the driving force.

To the mentors and thought leaders who paved the way, your contributions are recognized. And to the readers, your commitment to learning fuels the enduring relevance of this work.

This book stands as a testament to collaborative effort, aiming to inspire and empower generations of product managers.

With appreciation,
Abhishek

1 INTRODUCTION TO PRODUCT MANAGEMENT

In product management, numerous definitions abound, each attempting to encapsulate the essence of this multifaceted role. Some liken it to the position of a CEO, highlighting the profound value and influence product managers wield within the context of a product. However, it is crucial to discern that while product management and the CEO role share certain elements of strategic thinking and decision-making, their scope and responsibilities diverge significantly.

Debunking the CEO myth

At the apex of an organization's hierarchy, the CEO assumes the mantle of the highest-ranking executive, entrusted with steering the entire enterprise's course and performance. This overarching responsibility encompasses charting the company's vision and strategy, overseeing the day-to-day operations and financial matters, and making pivotal determinations regarding the enterprise's trajectory and focus.

Conversely, the product manager's domain is intricately tied to the development and prosperity of a particular product or product line within the organization's portfolio. Product managers are the architects of the product's vision and strategy, masters of crafting and prioritizing the product roadmap, and maestros in orchestrating the collaborative efforts of cross-functional teams. This includes close collaboration with departments such as engineering, design, sales, and marketing, all directed toward ensuring the product aligns seamlessly with customer needs and dovetails with the company's overarching objectives.

While the product manager's influence is indubitable and instrumental in shaping a product's success, their purview generally extends solely to the specific product or product line they steward. Conversely, the CEO shoulders a more expansive domain of responsibility, wielding a pivotal role in steering overall direction and strategic course of entire organization.

With this myth dispelled, let's delve deeper into intricate world of Product Management.

But first,

What exactly is Product Management?

Product Management constitutes comprehensive management of a product's development and lifecycle. This phase can span from its inception to its eventual retirement or even originate from a directive to forge something anew. The scope of product management is a fluid continuum without deterministic starting or concluding points. It operates within a dynamic realm of business, demanding prowess of strong leadership, effective communication, and adept problem-solving skills.

Curiously, despite the singular title of "product manager," a single product might find itself under the guidance of multiple stewards. This multiplicity unfolds in several possible scenarios:

1. Complexity: When a product is sprawling and intricate, comprising multiple teams or complex components, each facet may warrant dedicated product management. Here, individual product managers assume responsibility for distinct aspects or features of the product.

2. Multiple Teams: In cases where the product's development and management involve multiple teams or departments, each with its own specialized focus, the product may have a dedicated product manager for each unit. Consider a product jointly crafted and marketed by both a software team and a hardware team, each

necessitating its own product manager.

3. Lifecycle Handoff: Sometimes, a product transitions through various stages of its lifecycle, with different product managers at the helm. For instance, one product manager may be entrusted with defining the product's vision and strategic course, while another steers it through the intricacies of the product roadmap and its journey to market.

Irrespective of the scenario at play, it remains paramount for these product managers to collaborate closely and harmonize their efforts. This harmonization ensures that the product remains finely attuned to the ever-evolving needs of its customers and stays firmly aligned with the overarching goals and aspirations of the organization.

As succinctly summarized, "Sometimes product teams work in silos and develop their own roadmap that creates a user experience representing the internal product team rather than a seamless user experience on the product." Collaboration and coordination among product managers become the linchpin to counter such fragmentation and ensure a seamless user experience.

When people think of product management, it's common to conjure images of popular B2C (business-to-consumer) products like YouTube or TikTok. However, the scope of product management extends far beyond B2C offerings. There exists a substantial and thriving market for B2B (business-to-business) products that serve as platforms, empowering companies to develop their own products and services. These foundational products, often referred to as platform products, play a pivotal role in the business landscape.

What is a Platform Product

A platform product serves as the bedrock upon which other products or services are built. These products typically furnish a suite of tools, technologies, or infrastructure, enabling external entities—be they companies or individuals—to construct, deploy, or operate their distinct offerings atop the platform.

Examples of Platform Products

1. Operating Systems: Esteemed examples like Microsoft Windows or Apple's macOS provide the fundamental environment upon which a multitude of software applications operate.

2. Software Development Platforms: Widely adopted platforms like Microsoft's .NET or the Java platform equip developers with the resources necessary to create a vast array of software solutions.

3. Web-Based Platforms: Behemoths such as Meta (formerly Facebook) or Google's Android operating system offer a comprehensive ecosystem for developers and businesses to build and expand their online presence and services.

The Value of Platform Products

Platform products hold a distinct allure for businesses. They possess the capacity to generate continuous revenue streams through the products and services constructed upon them. Additionally, they can foster network effects, wherein the value of the platform appreciates in tandem with the growing ecosystem of products and services relying on it. This mutually beneficial dynamic drives innovation and expansion.

Challenges for Product Managers of Platform Products

Product managers tasked with nurturing platform products face a unique set of challenges. They must navigate the delicate balance of creating value for both the platform itself and the multitude of products and services woven into its fabric. This often involves harmonizing the needs and aspirations of diverse stakeholders, from the platform's users and developers to those of the overarching business objectives.

In essence, world of product management spans a broad spectrum, encompassing not only familiar B2C offerings but also dynamic and ever-evolving realm of B2B platform products. These foundational products underpin innovation and growth of countless businesses, embodying collaborative spirit of modern digital landscape.

Product management extends beyond the realm of direct product development in collaboration with engineering teams. In certain scenarios, an organization's objective revolves around amplifying product visibility and driving sales, necessitating a dedicated focus on stimulating demand and generating leads through marketing and sales initiatives. This is where the role of an outbound product manager comes into play—a pivotal figure in the pursuit of revenue and growth targets through the formulation and execution of outbound marketing and sales strategies aligned with overarching product and business objectives.

Outbound Product Management

This facet of product management is centered on igniting demand for a product and catalyzing lead generation and sales through an array of outbound marketing and sales avenues. These comprise diverse channels, such as advertising, content marketing, social media, email marketing, and proactive sales outreach. The role itself demands a fusion of robust marketing and sales competencies and an intimate comprehension of the target market's dynamics and the unique needs of customers.

Key Responsibilities: Outbound product managers assume the crucial responsibilities of identifying and precisely targeting the appropriate audience for the product. They craft persuasive messaging and positioning that resonates with the target audience, and they meticulously orchestrate marketing and sales campaigns designed to deliver tangible results.

In essence, the role of an outbound product manager stands as a linchpin in the pursuit of bridging the gap between product development and revenue generation. Their proficiency in understanding market dynamics, coupled with their adeptness in formulating and executing impactful marketing and sales initiatives, positions them as instrumental contributors to a company's growth and financial success.

Exercise to Identify your PM Quotient

You are the product manager for a mobile application that provides guided meditation and mindfulness exercises. Your app has been steadily growing its user base, but recently, you've noticed a decline in user engagement and retention. Users seem to download the app, try it for a few days, and then stop using it. You decide to investigate the issue and take action to improve user engagement and retention.

Question: Given the scenario, what should be your initial course of action as a product manager to address the declining user engagement and retention?

A) Immediately launch a new marketing campaign to attract more users to the app.

B) Analyze user data and conduct surveys or user interviews to understand why users are disengaging.

C) Redesign the entire user interface and introduce a fresh look to re-engage users.

D) Ignore the decline as it might be a temporary phase and continue with the existing strategy.

Please select the most appropriate option and provide a brief explanation for your choice.

Explanation: Option (B) is the correct course of action for a product manager facing declining user engagement and retention. Analyzing user data and gathering insights through surveys or interviews is a fundamental step in identifying the root causes of the problem. It allows the product manager to understand why users are disengaging and provides valuable information for making data-driven decisions to improve the app's user experience and content. Options (A), (C), and (D) do not address the core issue and may not lead to effective solutions.

Add your own text for the image.

2 PRODUCT STRATEGY

Engaging in the intricate process of product development requires a structured approach, delineated into seven distinct stages: planning, customer research, idea generation, concept development, prototyping, testing, and commercialization. These stages, meticulously organized, serve as a roadmap, substantially enhancing the prospects of a triumphant product launch. However, it is imperative to maintain awareness that the trajectory of product development is characterized by a requisite investment of time and patience. Success is contingent upon embracing the principles of customer-centricity, fostering innovation, cultivating adaptability, and exercising patience.

The Significance of Vision and Mission

During this intricate journey, the articulation of a clear vision and mission assumes paramount importance. These foundational elements not only serve as guiding principles but also as instruments for informed decision-making, talent acquisition, retention, and the ultimate realization of defined objectives.

Vision Statement: This succinct declaration encapsulates the lofty aspirations underlying the product's purpose. It furnishes a precise description of the product's raison d'être and ultimate destination.

Mission Statement: This articulates the core identity of the product and elucidates the tangible benefits it confers upon its users. A mission statement conveys the essential value proposition of the product.

Both the vision and mission statements demand conciseness, specificity, aspiration, and a foundation. They serve as sources of inspiration, directing the collective efforts of the team through the complex terrain of product development, guiding the attainment of well-defined goals.

Defining the Product Vision and Strategy

A product vision is akin to a grand aspiration or a significant concept—a mental image of what you aspire to create. Conversely, a strategy serves as the meticulously devised blueprint that transforms this vision into tangible reality. To illustrate this concept, envision your desire to construct a magnificent castle using building blocks. The vision represents the vivid mental picture of the castle, while the strategy outlines the step-by-step plan for its construction, encompassing the acquisition of the right blocks, their precise placement, and the meticulous attention to ensuring strength and stability. Following this strategy, one can discern the overarching investment themes needed to set the plan into motion.

Crucially, anchoring the product's vision to the enduring needs of customers is pivotal for long-term success within the market. A profound comprehension of your target customers' requirements, pain points, and aspirations serves as the compass that guides you towards innovative opportunities while ensuring that your product's vision remains harmoniously aligned with their needs. Once this understanding is attained, the groundwork for crafting your product vision begins. This vision should manifest as a clear and compelling statement, succinctly articulating what your product aspires to achieve and how it will enrich the lives of your customers. This process aligns with the wisdom of "beginning with the end in mind".

Here are some refined examples for inspiration:

1. "Our product endeavors to redefine personal finance management through an intuitive mobile app, simplifying budgeting, savings, and investment-all seamlessly integrated.

This empowers users with unparalleled control over their finances, propelling them towards their financial aspirations."

2. "Our product is dedicated to enhancing connections within busy families. Through our innovative family communication app, parents can effortlessly oversee their children's schedules, share crucial information, and maintain familial bonds, even amidst their hectic lives. This bestows upon customers the gift of peace of mind, fostering organization and family togetherness."

3. "Our product is poised to transform grocery shopping. It introduces an online platform that affords customers the convenience of shopping from home, with doorstep delivery. This invaluable service saves customers time, eliminates hassle, and elevates the entire grocery shopping experience."

4. "Our product is pioneering a new era of online security. We present a cutting-edge VPN service, fortifying your online presence through comprehensive data encryption, safeguarding your digital privacy, and shielding you from the ever-present specter of cyber threats. This ensures customers can navigate the online realm with unwavering confidence in their security."

These statements maintain clarity and conviction by delineating precisely what the product seeks to achieve and the tangible advantages it confers upon its users. They harness persuasive language and underscore the distinctive value proposition that the product brings to its customers.

However, crafting a product vision can prove to be a formidable task for product managers, as it necessitates an in-depth comprehension of the market, the customers, and prevailing industry trends. Devoid of a profound understanding of these critical factors, product managers may encounter challenges in spotting opportunities for innovation and formulating a vision that harmonizes with customer needs.

To aid in the creation of a clear and captivating product vision, several techniques are at your disposal. Here are a few illustrative exercises that can facilitate the development of a compelling product vision:

Hands-on Exercises

1. Customer Journey Mapping: Construct a visual representation of the customer's voyage, encompassing the pain points and requisites they encounter before, during, and after engaging with your product. Leverage this mapping to unearth innovative prospects and shape a vision that addresses these pain points effectively.

2. Value Proposition Canvas: Employ a value proposition canvas to pinpoint the distinct value your product will deliver to customers. This exercise aids in defining a vision that succinctly communicates how your product will enrich the lives of its users.

3. Innovation Games: Engage in innovation games like "crazy 8s" or "what if" to spark a profusion of ideas for novel products or features. Harness these creative concepts to mold a vision that stands out as genuinely unique and pioneering.

4. Future Scenario Planning: Envision diverse future scenarios in which your product can provide solutions. Consider the potential impact and benefits your product might offer in these scenarios. This strategic exercise nurtures a forward-thinking vision that considers evolving market needs.

Example

Let's say you are developing a product that aims to make grocery shopping more convenient for busy families.

1. Customer journey mapping: You map out the typical customer journey, including the pain points they experience, such as long lines, busy parking lots, and difficulty finding products. Your product vision is to create an innovative grocery shopping experience that is fast, easy, and convenient for busy families.

2. Value proposition canvas: You identify that your product's unique value is that it will save customers time and hassle by allowing them to shop for groceries online and have them delivered to their door. Your product vision is to revolutionize

the way busy families shop for groceries by providing a convenient and time-saving online shopping experience.

3. Innovation games: You use an innovation game like "crazy 8s" to generate a wide range of ideas for new products or features. One idea is to create an app that uses AI to make personalized grocery suggestions for each customer, based on their previous purchases and preferences. Your product vision is to use cutting-edge technology to create a personalized and convenient grocery shopping experience for customers.

4. Future scenario planning: You imagine a scenario in the future where smart homes are more common, and your product vision is to develop a platform that allows customers to easily order groceries through their smart home devices and have them delivered within an hour.

Competition

While product managers like to focus on customers, competition also plays an important role in defining a product vision. It is important for product managers to understand the competitive landscape to identify opportunities for innovation and to develop a unique and compelling vision for their product. Knowing the competition can help a product manager understand what is currently available in the market, what are the current trends, and what are the gaps in the market. This understanding can be used to develop a vision that is differentiated from the competition and that addresses the needs of customers in a unique way.

Additionally, understanding the competition can also help product managers set realistic and achievable goals for their product. By understanding what the competition is offering and what their strengths and weaknesses are, product managers can set goals that are ambitious but still achievable. One practical way to conduct a competitive analysis is by using publicly available tools and resources.

The first step in this process is to identify your competitors. You can do this by searching for companies and products that offer similar solutions to yours. Websites like Google, LinkedIn, and Crunchbase are great places to start. Once you've identified your competitors, gather information about them using publicly available resources such as their website, press releases, and industry reports. You can also use tools such as SEMrush, Ahrefs, and SimilarWeb to gather information about your competitors' traffic, keywords, and backlinks.

With the information you've gathered, you can then analyze the strengths and weaknesses of your competitors. Look at their product features, pricing, distribution channels, marketing strategies, and overall competitiveness in the market. Tools such as Crayon and Owler can help you gather information about your competitors' funding, revenue, and employee count.

Furthermore, it is important to identify the opportunities and threats that your competitors pose to your business. Look for areas where your competitors are not currently serving customers or where they have a weak presence and consider how you can take advantage of these opportunities. Additionally, determining the positioning of your competitors in the market by analyzing their branding and messaging can be done by using tools such as Brand24 and Mention to track mentions of your competitors' brand and products across social media, blogs, and forums.

Lastly, it is important to monitor and review your competitors regularly. Use tools such as Google Alerts and Mention to stay informed of any changes or new developments in the market. By conducting a competitive analysis using publicly available tools and resources, you can gain a better understanding of the competitive landscape, identify opportunities for innovation, and develop a unique and compelling vision for your product.

Blue Ocean and Red Ocean

Two potent strategies, known as the Blue Ocean and Red Ocean strategies, offer distinct routes for balancing innovation and competition.

Before we delve into practical implementation, let's establish a clear understanding of Blue Ocean and Red Ocean strategies:

- Blue Ocean Strategy: Imagine carving out a unique market space where competition is minimal. The Blue Ocean Strategy advocates creating a niche by offering a product or service that is radically innovative and distinct from existing offerings. It's centered on value innovation, where differentiation and cost-effectiveness are pursued concurrently.

- Red Ocean Strategy: Conversely, the Red Ocean is the competitive battleground within established markets. Success here necessitates gaining a competitive edge within the confines of existing industries. Factors such as pricing, quality, and marketing become the focal points of competition.

Initiating Blue Ocean Thinking

1. Identify Untapped Markets: Commence by identifying markets or customer segments with low competition. Seek out unmet needs, pain points, or market gaps where existing solutions fall short.

2. Prioritize Innovation and Differentiation: Develop a product vision rooted in innovation and distinctiveness. Focus on creating a unique value proposition that differentiates your offering from competitors.

3. Embrace Value Innovation: Value innovation is the cornerstone of the Blue Ocean Strategy—creating fresh value for customers while simultaneously reducing costs. Achieve this through inventive features, pricing strategies, user experiences, or business models.

4. Thorough Market Research: Dive into comprehensive market research to validate your Blue Ocean opportunities. Analyze customer preferences, demand trends, and the potential for market adoption.

5. Prototyping and Validation: Validate your concept by rapidly prototyping and testing it with potential users. Gather feedback and refine your approach accordingly.

Transitioning to Red Ocean Execution

1. Competitive Analysis: Transition into a Red Ocean mindset by

conducting an in-depth analysis of the competitive landscape within your selected market.

2. Competitor Evaluation: Assess competitors meticulously—identify their strengths and vulnerabilities. Gain insights into their pricing strategies, product features, and marketing tactics.

3. Strategic Positioning and Pricing: Based on your competitive analysis, devise a strategy for positioning your product effectively. Determine pricing strategies aligned with your product's unique value proposition and competitive advantages.

4. Strategic Marketing: Craft marketing strategies that emphasize your product's distinctive attributes while addressing customer pain points. Leverage the differentiation you've cultivated through Blue Ocean thinking.

5. Continuous Adaptation: In the Red Ocean, adaptability is vital. Continuously monitor market dynamics and competitors' actions, and collect customer feedback to refine your product and strategy.

Seamless Integration of Both Strategies

- Hybrid Strategy: Consider adopting a hybrid approach that blends elements of both Blue Ocean and Red Ocean strategies. Innovate in certain areas (Blue Ocean) while optimizing efficiency and cost-effectiveness in others (Red Ocean).

- Diverse Product Portfolio: Maintain a balanced product portfolio that encompasses both innovative, Blue Ocean products and those catering to established markets (Red Ocean). This diversification hedges risks and ensures a steady revenue stream.

- Iterative Business Approach: Product management is characterized by ongoing iteration. Continuously assess your product's performance and adapt your strategic approach between Blue Ocean and Red Ocean strategies as circumstances dictate.

Once you have developed a clear and compelling product vision, the next step is to develop a product strategy to achieve that vision.

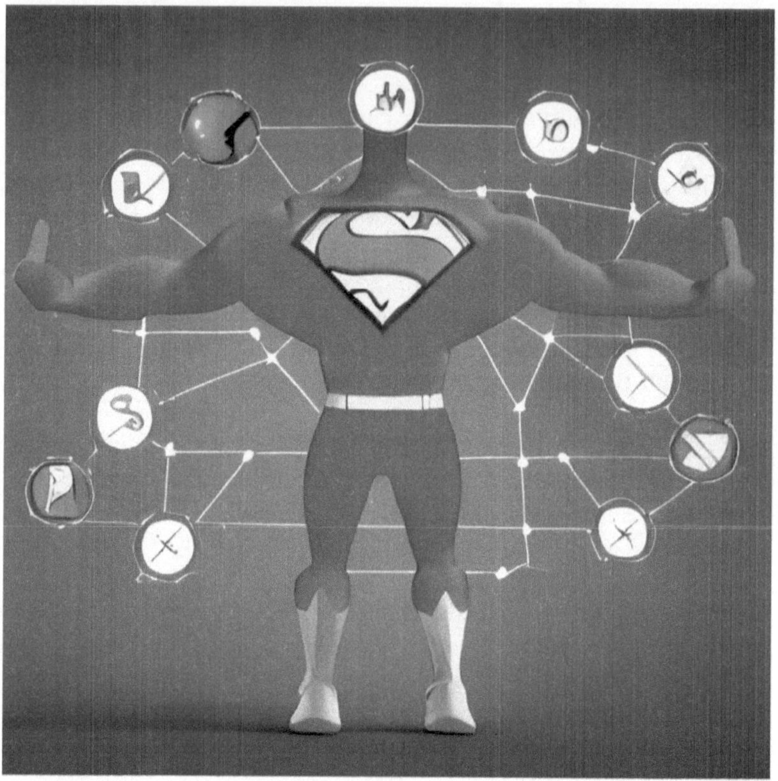

Identify the elements in the above image.

Alright, let's get started on defining our product strategy to achieve our vision.

First things first, who are our target customers? We need to understand their needs, pain points, and desires like we understand our own. We can conduct market research, customer interviews, and surveys to gain a deep understanding of our target market. And remember, if we don't know who we're building this product for, we'll end up creating something that nobody wants, and that's no fun!

Next, we need to set some specific, measurable, and achievable goals and objectives for our product. These goals should align with our product vision and be focused on delivering value to our target market. It's important to establish clear and measurable targets, such as increasing customer satisfaction by X% or achieving Y in revenue. Without clear goals, we'll be just shooting arrows in the dark, and that's never a good idea.

Then, we need to develop a unique value proposition that clearly communicates the benefits of our product and how it addresses the needs of our target market. A unique value proposition is like a superhero's motto; it tells the customers how we're different from the competition and how we're going to save the day. Without a unique value proposition, we'll just be another superhero without a costume, and that's not a pretty sight.

After that, we need to identify the key features and functionality that our product must have to achieve its vision and deliver value to our target market. This step is like building a superhero's suit; we need to make sure that it's able to deliver on its promise and meet the needs of the target market.

Then, we create a roadmap that outlines the steps that need to be taken to achieve our product vision and goals. A roadmap is like a superhero's map; it shows the path to success and helps to communicate the plan to different stakeholders.

Next, we measure the progress against our defined success criteria. It helps us determine the progress of the product and ensure that it is on track to achieve its goals.

An example of a product strategy that can be used as a template for delivering a web application that helps users increase their productivity by providing an easy-to-use interface, integrating with popular calendar and email apps, and providing a premium subscription with additional features. The strategy also aligns with the company's overall strategy and has clear goals and objectives for user engagement, revenue, and customer satisfaction.

Write the name of each stakeholder in the image.

Product Strategy Template

1. Target Market:
    - Young professionals in the age range of 25-40 who use the internet regularly.
    - Customers who want to stay organized, stay on top of their tasks, and increase their productivity.
    - Market research and customer feedback analysis have shown that there is a high demand for a web application that can help users manage their tasks and increase their productivity.

2. Goals and Objectives:
    - Increase user engagement by 30% within the first 6 months of launch.

- Achieve 1 million registered users within the first year of launch.
- Increase customer satisfaction by 20% within the first year of launch.
- Increase revenue by 15% within the first year of launch.

3. Unique Value Proposition:
   - Our web application offers a simple, user-friendly interface that helps users stay organized and increase their productivity.
   - Our web application integrates with popular calendar and email apps, making it easy for users to manage their tasks and schedule.
   - Our web application offers a premium subscription that includes additional features and functionalities to help users increase their productivity.

4. Key Features and Functionality:
   - Task management and scheduling
   - Integration with popular calendar and email apps
   - Premium subscription that includes additional features and functionalities
   - User-friendly interface
   - Personalization options
   - Cloud-based storage

5. Roadmap:
   - Phase 1 (within 6 months of launch): Release basic task management and scheduling features
   - Phase 2 (within 12 months of launch): Release integration with popular calendar and email apps
   - Phase 3 (within 18 months of launch): Release a premium subscription with additional features and functionalities.

6. Metrics and Success Criteria:
   - Number of registered users
   - User engagement (measured by active users and average session duration)
   - Customer satisfaction (measured by customer feedback and a survey)

- Revenue

7. Alignment with the Company's Strategy:
   - Align with the company's overall strategy of providing innovative and user-friendly web applications that help users increase their productivity.
   - Get buy-in from relevant departments (marketing, development, customer service).

8. Communication and Stakeholder Management:
   - Regular communication with stakeholders (team, other departments, and leadership)
   - Get buy-in and feedback from key stakeholders to ensure alignment with the needs of the company and the market.

When it comes to creating a successful product, it's not just about building something cool and hoping for the best. It's also about aligning our product strategy with the company's overall strategy and goals.

Before delving into product prioritization, it's crucial to establish an effective mechanism for implementing the review of the strategy document, ensuring seamless alignment among different teams with the broader vision.

Mechanism: OP1/OP2

Organizations often employ planning cycles, commonly known as OP1 and OP2 (OP stands for Operational Planning), to foster a bottom-up culture. In these cycles, individual product teams are empowered to create their own strategy documents. These team-specific strategies serve as valuable blueprints that reflect the unique nuances and objectives of each team.

The first of these cycles, OP1, typically occurs on an annual basis. During this time, teams engage in a comprehensive review of their strategies, carefully examining their goals, priorities, and resource requirements for the upcoming year. It's a holistic assessment that allows teams to refine their strategies and chart their course in alignment with the organization's overarching vision.

However, strategic alignment is an ongoing endeavor, and waiting a full year to synchronize efforts may not suffice. This is where OP2 comes into play, positioned as a mid-year checkpoint occurring every six months. OP2 serves as a dynamic space for teams to revisit and adapt their strategies in response to evolving market dynamics or shifting priorities. It also provides an opportunity for recalibrating resource allocation to ensure that teams have the necessary talent and capacity to execute their strategies effectively.

In this approach, the strategies developed by individual teams are not isolated endeavors but integral components of a broader, cohesive organizational strategy. The culmination of these team-specific strategies, reviewed, refined, and consolidated through OP1 and OP2 cycles, forms the overarching strategy document for the entire division. This harmonized strategy is a testament to the organization's commitment to adaptability, alignment, and the pursuit of a shared vision.

3 KNOW YOUR CUSTOMERS

To write a good strategy document for the product, we must start with our customers. It begins by understanding their pain points and desires, and then crafting a product that directly addresses these needs. This process involves working backward, starting with the end goal firmly in mind.

Customer Interviews

Customer interviews are a cornerstone of effective product management. As a product manager, it's essential to acknowledge that you can't be an expert in every domain your product touches. This is where customer interviews come into play. Customers are the true experts when it comes to their own needs, challenges, and preferences. By engaging in one-on-one conversations with them, you gain deep insights into their specific problems and the emotional impact these issues have on their experiences.

Moreover, customer interviews uncover unmet needs that may not be immediately apparent through technical or data-driven analysis. While customers may not always provide explicit solutions, they can articulate their pain points and aspirations, which can lead to innovative product features or improvements.

Beyond insights, customer interviews also help build empathy. Empathy is a fundamental aspect of effective product management. These interviews allow you to step into your users' shoes, understand their motivations, and appreciate their frustrations. This empathy not only fuels your passion for creating products that resonate but also ensures that your decisions are rooted in a genuine understanding of your audience.

Additionally, customer interviews play a crucial role in validating assumptions. Product managers often make assumptions about what customers want or need. Customer interviews provide an opportunity to test these assumptions, ensuring that your product roadmap is based on actual user feedback rather than conjecture.

In addition to customer interviews, data-driven development is another essential aspect of modern product management. Data provides a factual basis for decision-making, which is crucial for making informed choices about feature prioritization, resource allocation, and product optimization. Regularly collecting and analyzing data enables you to spot areas for enhancement and make incremental changes to your product over time, ensuring that it remains competitive and relevant.

Data-driven development also emphasizes the measurement of impact. When you launch new features or changes, data allows you to objectively measure their effects. By tracking key performance indicators (KPIs), you can determine whether your initiatives are driving the desired outcomes or if adjustments are needed.

Write the conversation for the image.

Moreover, A/B testing is a powerful technique within the realm of data-driven development. By comparing the performance of different versions of your product, you can identify what resonates most with your users and fine-tune your offering accordingly.

Lastly, data-driven development enables you to adapt swiftly to market shifts and changing user preferences. Markets evolve, and data-driven insights help you pivot your product strategy when necessary, ensuring its long-term viability and relevance.

After customer interviews, creating personas provides a clear representation of the target user who emerged from the interviews. It highlights her goals, needs, pain points, and the tech stack she relies on. Product managers can use this persona as a reference point when making decisions about feature prioritization, user experience design, and product development to ensure that the product aligns with Sarah's specific needs and preferences.

Understanding your customers is only half the battle; the real magic happens when you apply what you've learned to create exceptional products.

You've conducted insightful customer interviews and collected a wealth of data, and now it's time to translate those valuable insights into actionable steps for your product development. This is where the art of crafting effective user stories comes into play. User stories are a critical component of agile development and serve as a bridge between customer needs and product features.

Here's how to use your newfound insights to create user stories that drive your product forward.

Creating User Stories

1. Start with clear goals.

Begin by revisiting your interview objectives and the insights you've gathered. What are the key pain points and desires that emerged from the interviews? Your user stories should align with these findings and help address specific customer needs. For example, if customers expressed frustration with a cumbersome login process, a user story might begin like this:

As a [user type], I want to [perform an action] so that [achieve a specific goal].

- As a frequent customer,
- I want to be able to log in using my fingerprint.
- so that I can access my account quickly and securely.

2. Focus on user personas.

Your customer interviews likely revealed various user personas with distinct needs and preferences. Tailor your user stories to cater to these personas. Consider creating different stories for different user types, ensuring that each story addresses their unique pain points. This approach ensures that your product caters to a diverse user base. For instance:

As a [persona], I want to [perform an action] so that [achieve a specific goal].

- As a busy professional,
- I want to receive push notifications for new messages.
- so that I can stay updated on important communications while on the go.

3. Be specific and action oriented.

Avoid vague or generic user stories. They should clearly articulate what needs to be done and why. Use specific action verbs to describe the user's actions and the desired outcome. This clarity helps your development team understand the user's perspective. For example:

As a [user type], I want to [perform a specific action] so that [achieve a specific benefit].

- As a movie enthusiast,
- I want to filter search results by genre.
- so that I can quickly find movies that match my preferences.

4. Include acceptance criteria.

To prevent ambiguity and ensure a shared understanding, include acceptance criteria for each user story. These criteria define the conditions that must be met for the story to be considered complete. They often take the form of "Given-When-Then" statements. For instance:

Given [initial context], when [specific action], then [expected outcome].

- Given that the user is logged in, when they click the "Add to Cart" button, the item should be added to their shopping cart.

5. Prioritize based on impact.

Not all user stories are created equal. Prioritize them based on the impact they will have on your users and business goals. The insights from your interviews should help you identify which stories address critical pain points or offer significant value. Prioritization ensures that your development team focuses on the most important features first. We will cover prioritization in detail later in the chapter.

6. Iterate and refine.

Customer insights are not static. As you continue to gather feedback and conduct more interviews, be prepared to iterate on your user stories. Refine them to reflect evolving customer needs and changing priorities. Agile development encourages flexibility and adaptability, so don't hesitate to adjust your stories as necessary.

By harnessing the power of customer insights in your user stories, you bridge the gap between understanding your users and delivering products that truly resonate with them. This user-centric approach not only drives product success but also fosters customer loyalty and advocacy.

Examples

Here are a few additional examples of good user stories:

1. "As a busy professional, I want a calendar feature that syncs with my work and personal schedules so that I can easily see all of my appointments in one place."

2. "As a frequent traveler, I want a mobile app that allows me to book flights, hotels, and rental cars in one place, so that I can easily plan and book my trips."

3. "As a student, I want a note-taking app that allows me to take notes, highlight important text, and organize my notes by class or subject, so that I can stay organized and study more effectively."

4. "As a small business owner, I want an invoicing and payment system that allows me to create and send invoices to my clients, track payments, and manage my finances, so that I can focus on running my business."

User stories are brief, simple descriptions of a feature or capability that a product should provide, written from the perspective of the user. Product managers then prioritize the user stories based on their importance to the target market and their potential impact on the business. This can help product managers focus on the most valuable and impactful features and capabilities first.

Need for Grouping User Stories into Themes

In the dynamic field of product management, user stories represent the heartbeat of your development process. While each user story is a vital component on its own, their collective arrangement into themes is the art of strategic planning that amplifies the impact of your product development efforts. In this section, we'll explore why themes are pivotal, especially when viewed through the lens of Jobs-to-Be-Done (JTBD), and offer a comprehensive guide on how to incorporate them effectively into your product management journey.

Write user stories for the pieces that form themes as per shade.

Why Themes Matter in the Context of JTBD

1. Alignment with Customer Needs

Themes facilitate the alignment of your product development with customer needs, or "jobs" in JTBD terminology. By clustering related user stories within themes, you ensure that your product enhancements are purpose-driven and directly tied to addressing specific jobs or tasks that customers are trying to accomplish. This alignment not only enhances user satisfaction but also bolsters customer loyalty, as you're focused on helping them achieve their desired outcomes.

2. Effective Prioritization

Effective prioritization is the linchpin of successful product development, and JTBD provides a clear framework for this. Themes play a crucial role in this regard by helping you categorize user stories according to their importance in fulfilling customer jobs. With JTBD, you can discern which jobs are more critical to your users and prioritize themes accordingly. This optimizes resource allocation and time management, ensuring that you're addressing the most pressing customer needs first.

3. Consistency and Coherence

Consistency and coherence in your product are non-negotiable for a superior user experience, a key principle in JTBD. Themes contribute to this by grouping related user stories that collectively address the same job. When these stories are developed together, they're more likely to work seamlessly, resulting in a unified and satisfying user journey that aligns with the customer's job execution.

4. Clear Communication

Themes, when framed within the context of JTBD, are instrumental in communicating a clear product vision focused on helping customers get their jobs done more efficiently. They encapsulate the strategic direction of your product and ensure that every stakeholder understands how individual user stories contribute to the overarching mission of facilitating specific jobs. This clarity fosters a sense of purpose, enhances collaboration, and aligns everyone towards a common goal: improving the customers' ability to accomplish their jobs.

5. Collaboration and Knowledge Sharing

Themes encourage collaboration across cross-functional teams, which is pivotal when leveraging JTBD insights. When multiple teams are aligned on working towards a common theme centered around solving specific jobs, they can share knowledge, coordinate efforts, and ensure that all elements of the theme are developed cohesively. This synergy prevents disjointed user experiences and promotes a unified product, resulting in smoother job execution for customers.

Practical Approach: Consider how Kuber applied JTBD. They didn't just create a ride-hailing app; they understood the "job" customers wanted to accomplish convenient, affordable transportation. Kuber's success comes from continuously enhancing the progress (efficiency) and outcomes (safety, reliability) of this job.

Implementing Themes with JTBD and Examples

Now that we've established the significance of themes, especially when viewed through the JTBD lens, let's explore how to effectively implement them within your product development process:

1. Identify common jobs-to-be-done threads.

Begin by scrutinizing your collected user stories through the JTBD framework. Look for common jobs or tasks that customers are trying to accomplish, patterns in how they execute these jobs, and any recurring pain points they face. These commonalities serve as the foundation for your themes, which are essentially focused on improving how customers accomplish their jobs.

Example: Through customer interviews, you discover that users frequently struggle with the "Hiring a Contractor" job, which includes finding, vetting, and hiring a service provider. This common job execution issue forms the basis for the "Streamlined Contractor Hiring" theme.

2. Define the objectives in the context of JTBD.

For each theme, define clear and concise objectives with a JTBD perspective in mind. What specific improvements or solutions will this theme encompass that directly aid customers in executing their jobs more effectively? Establishing these objectives ensures that your theme has a defined purpose and measurable outcomes tied to job execution improvements.

Example: The "Streamlined Contractor Hiring" theme aims to

reduce the time and effort required for customers to find, vet, and hire a service provider for their home improvement needs.

3. Organize individual user stories within each theme while keeping the JTBD perspective in mind.

Each user story should align with and contribute to achieving the objectives set for the theme, ensuring that every aspect of the theme serves a purpose directly related to improving job execution.

Example: User stories within the "Streamlined Contractor Hiring" theme may include "As a homeowner, I want to easily access ratings and reviews of contractors" and "As a homeowner, I want a simplified way to request and compare quotes from contractors." These user stories directly address pain points within the "Hiring a Contractor" job.

Outcomes-based approach

For effective prioritization, once you've defined the core job, you need to identify the outcomes that customers desire when they successfully complete that job. Outcomes can be categorized into different types:

Core Outcome:

- Functional outcome: This is the primary and most tangible outcome directly related to accomplishing the core job. It answers the question, "What does the customer achieve functionally when the job is done?" For example, if the core job is "finding a convenient transportation option," the core outcome could be "reaching a destination quickly and safely."

Secondary Outcomes:

- Efficiency outcomes: These outcomes relate to saving time, effort, or resources. Customers may desire efficient outcomes when completing a job. For instance, finding a transportation option quickly without searching extensively.

- Effectiveness outcomes: These outcomes are about achieving a higher level of quality, accuracy, or effectiveness in completing the job. For example, customers might want a transportation option that offers a smooth and comfortable ride.

Emotional and Social Outcomes:

- Emotional outcomes: Consider the emotional states customers desire when completing the job. For example, finding a transportation option might provide peace of mind, reducing the stress associated with commuting.

- Social outcomes: Explore how customers' social status or relationships might be affected by completing the job. For instance, using a trendy transportation service might enhance a customer's social image.

JTBD is not a one-time exercise; it's an ongoing process. Continuously monitor customer feedback, track key performance indicators (KPIs), and adapt your product based on changing customer needs and evolving outcomes. Iterate and refine your product to ensure it remains aligned with the JTBD.

In summary, associating outcomes with JTBD is a crucial step in creating products that truly meet customer needs. By understanding the core job and the desired outcomes, you can design, market, and improve your product to provide a holistic solution that resonates with your target audience.

Additional Reading

Sample persona Let's create a persona for our hypothetical product based on the insights gained from those interviews.

Persona: Sarah, the Busy Professional

Background:
Sarah is a 32-year-old marketing manager at a mid-sized tech company. She's a highly motivated and busy professional, juggling multiple responsibilities at work and home. Sarah is tech-savvy and values efficiency in her daily life.

Goals and Needs:

1. Time Efficiency: Sarah's top priority is to save time wherever possible. She's always on the lookout for tools and solutions that can streamline her work processes, allowing her to focus on strategic tasks.

2. Data-Driven Decision Making: As a marketing manager, Sarah relies heavily on data to make informed decisions. She seeks products that provide accurate, real-time analytics and insights to optimize her marketing campaigns.

3. Flexibility: Sarah often works remotely and needs tools that are accessible from anywhere. Flexibility in terms of device compatibility and cloud-based features is crucial to her.

4. Effective Communication: Sarah collaborates with cross-functional teams and clients regularly. She values products that facilitate smooth communication, whether through integrated messaging or collaborative project management features.

Pain Points:

1. Time Constraints: Sarah often finds herself overwhelmed with tight deadlines and a demanding workload. Any product that doesn't help her save time or adds complexity is a significant pain point.

2. Data Discrepancies: Inaccurate or delayed data reporting frustrates Sarah, as it hampers her ability to make data-driven decisions.

3. Limited Mobility: Products that don't support remote work or lack mobile app options hinder Sarah's productivity.

4. Communication Barriers: Poor communication tools or platforms that don't integrate well with her existing workflow disrupt Sarah's collaborative efforts.

Tech Stack:

- CRM software for managing client relationships

- Email marketing tools for campaign execution

- Project management software for team collaboration

- Data analytics platforms for performance tracking

Quote

> "Time is my most valuable resource. I need tools that not only simplify my workload but also empower me with real-time data and the flexibility to work from anywhere. Communication and collaboration should be effortless, so I can focus on driving results for my team."

In the world of product management, one skill stands out as an absolute must-have: the ability to conduct insightful and impactful customer interviews. As a product manager, your success hinges on your capacity to understand your customers' needs, preferences, and pain points. In this chapter, we will guide you through the art of conducting customer interviews that yield valuable insights.

Preparing for the Customer Interview

Before diving into interviews, careful preparation is essential. Think of it as the foundation upon which your interview success rests. Your preparation should include:

Defining Objectives

Clearly articulate your goals and objectives for the interview. What specific information are you seeking to gather? What decisions will this data influence?

Selecting the Right Participants

Identify the individuals who will provide the most relevant insights. This involves considering demographics, roles, and their relationship to your product or service.

Setting Up the Interview

Consider logistics such as scheduling and location. Ensure the interview environment is comfortable and conducive to open conversation.

Creating a Structured Interview Guide

A well-structured interview guide is your roadmap for the conversation. Craft open-ended questions that encourage meaningful responses. Here are a few pointers:

Open-Ended Questions

Design questions that encourage detailed responses. Avoid yes-or-no questions. For instance, ask "Can you describe your daily workflow?" instead of "Do you like our product?"

Sample Questions

Here are some examples of effective interview questions for various situations:

- "What challenges do you face in your daily work?"

- "Tell me about your experience using our product."

- "How would you improve our service if you had a magic wand?"

Adaptability

Remember that your interview guide is a flexible tool. Be prepared to adapt and ask follow-up questions based on the interviewee's responses.

Building Rapport

Building a rapport with your interviewees is vital. It fosters trust and creates an environment where participants are more likely to share candid insights. Techniques for achieving this include:

Establishing Trust

Start the interview with a friendly introduction and an icebreaker. Create an atmosphere where interviewees feel safe and comfortable.

Active Listening

Practice active listening to demonstrate that you value their input. Reflect on their responses, ask clarifying questions, and show empathy.

Conducting the Interview

Now, let's dive into the interview itself. Here's how you can ensure a productive and insightful conversation:

Icebreakers and introductions

Begin with a warm welcome and a brief introduction. Icebreakers help ease tension and set a positive tone for the interview.

Asking questions

Pose open-ended questions, allowing interviewees to share their thoughts freely. Encourage them to elaborate and provide examples.

Handling challenges

Be prepared for unexpected challenges during the interview, such as resistance or incomplete answers. Stay patient and adapt your approach as needed.

Analyzing and synthesizing data

Effective notetaking is crucial during interviews. Afterward, the collected data must be carefully analyzed and synthesized. Here's how:

Note-taking

During the interview, record key points, quotes, and observations. Ensure your notes capture the essence of the conversation.

Data analysis

Once the interviews are complete, analyse the data to identify patterns and trends. Look for common pain points, desires, and preferences.

Distilling insights

From your analysis, distil actionable insights. These should inform your product decisions and future iterations.

4 PRIOTIZATIONS

Now that we've established the power of user stories and the strategic value of themes in guiding your product development, it's time to tackle a critical aspect of the process: prioritization. Prioritization is the compass that guides your product roadmap, ensuring that you focus on what matters most to your customers and business goals. In this section, we'll delve into why prioritization is crucial and offer strategies to prioritize user stories and themes effectively.

The Significance of Prioritization

1. Maximizing impact

Effective prioritization ensures that you're working on the most impactful user stories and themes first. It allows you to address the pain points and needs that have the greatest influence on your users' satisfaction and retention. By tackling high-impact items early, you can deliver value sooner and start reaping the benefits sooner.

2. Aligning with business objectives

Prioritization helps you align your product development efforts with your broader business objectives. It ensures that the features and improvements you work on are directly tied to strategic goals such as revenue growth, customer acquisition, or market expansion. This alignment is essential for demonstrating the value of your product to stakeholders.

3. Efficient resource allocation

In the world of product management, resources are finite. Prioritization allows you to allocate these resources efficiently. By focusing on the most critical user stories and themes, you make the best use of your development team's time and expertise. This not only enhances productivity but also optimizes your budget and timeline.

4. Managing risk

Prioritization helps you manage risk effectively. By addressing high-risk user stories and themes early, you can identify potential challenges and uncertainties sooner in the development process. This allows you to mitigate risks proactively, reducing the likelihood of costly setbacks or surprises later.

5. Iteration and learning

A well-prioritized product roadmap supports an iterative and learning-driven approach. It acknowledges that not all user stories or themes will be perfect on the first attempt.

Prioritization enables you to gather feedback quickly and make necessary adjustments, fostering continuous improvement and adaptation to changing customer needs.

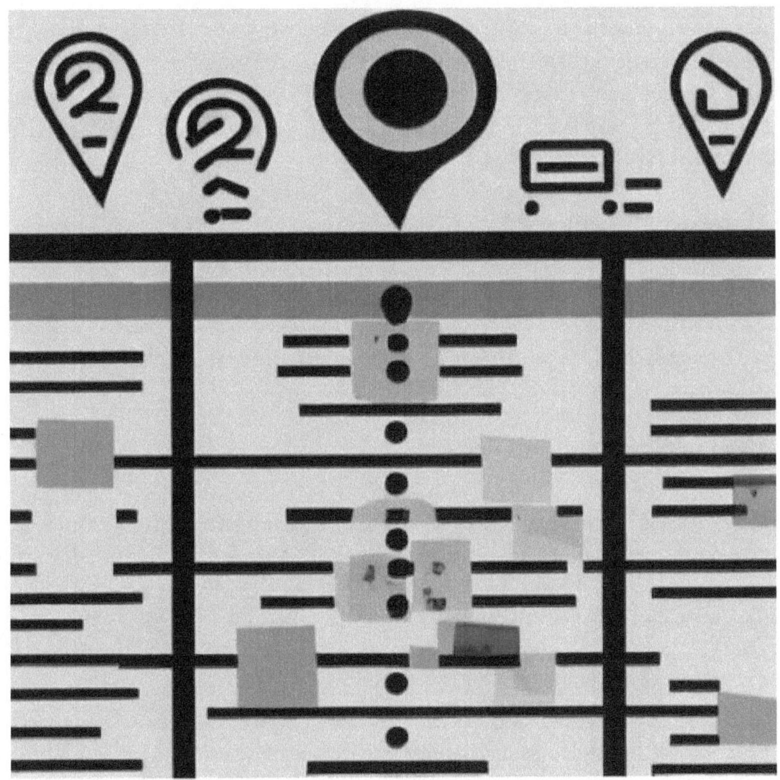

In the image, write the tasks and user stories arranged in order of priority, symbolizing their importance. Show how prioritization ensures that you focus on what matters most to customers and business goals.

Strategies for Prioritization: Leveraging Frameworks

1. Impact vs. Effort Analysis

One common approach is to assess user stories and themes based on their expected impact on users or business objectives versus the effort required to implement them. This approach is often used in conjunction with the MoSCoW framework.

2. Customer Feedback and Pain Points

Consider feedback from customer interviews and user research. Prioritize user stories and themes that directly address pain points and desires expressed by your users. These are often the most compelling areas for improvement, as emphasized in the Jobs-to-Be-Done (JTBD) framework.

3. Jobs-to-be-Done (JTBD) Significance

If you've applied the JTBD framework to your themes, prioritize themes that focus on jobs that are central to your users' needs. These are typically high-priority areas where customers are seeking efficient solutions.

4. MoSCoW Method

The MoSCoW method categorises user stories and themes into four categories: must-haves, should-haves, could-haves, and won't-haves. This framework helps prioritize items based on their criticality and importance.

5. Kano Model

The Kano Model classifies user stories and themes into different categories based on their impact on customer satisfaction, including basic needs, performance Needs, and excitement needs. Prioritization is driven by the category of needs that each item fulfils.

6. Value vs. Complexity Matrix

A value vs. complexity matrix assesses user stories and themes by plotting their potential value against the complexity of implementation. This visual representation helps prioritize items that offer the most significant value with manageable complexity.

7. RICE Framework

The RICE framework combines reach, impact, confidence, and effort to score user stories and themes. It provides a numerical score that aids in prioritizing items based on their potential impact and feasibility.

8. Weighted Scoring

Create a scoring system that assigns weights to different factors, such as customer impact, business value, technical complexity, and strategic alignment. Calculate scores for each user story and theme to guide prioritization decisions.

Impact versus Effort Analysis

One of the most fundamental and widely used methods for prioritizing user stories and themes is Impact versus effort analysis. This approach provides a structured framework to evaluate potential improvements or features based on two critical dimensions: their expected impact on the product or business and the effort required for their implementation. By plotting these factors on a graph or matrix, you can make informed decisions about where to allocate your resources and focus your development efforts most effectively.

Understanding the Dimensions

1. Impact

The impact dimension represents the expected benefit or value that a user story or theme will deliver when implemented. It is essential to consider both the magnitude of the impact and who will benefit from it. Impact can manifest in various forms, including:

- Customer Satisfaction: Will it significantly improve the user experience or address a critical pain point for your customers?

- Revenue Generation: Can it lead to increased sales, customer retention, or new revenue streams?

- Market Competitiveness: Will it enhance your product's position in the market and give you a competitive edge?

- Strategic Alignment: Does it align with your long-term

business objectives and product vision?

2. Effort

Effort represents the resources required to design, develop, test, and deploy a user story or theme. This dimension encompasses factors such as:

*   Development Time: How long will it take to implement the feature or improvement? Consider both the duration of development and any associated tasks like testing and quality assurance.

*   Complexity: Is it technically challenging to implement? Does it involve significant changes to the existing codebase or infrastructure?

*   Resource Allocation: How many team members and what skill sets are needed to complete the work?

*   Cost: What are the financial implications of dedicating resources to this task?

Creating an Impact vs. Effort Matrix

To conduct an impact versus effort analysis effectively, follow these steps:

1. Identify user stories or themes.

Start by listing the user stories or themes you want to evaluate for prioritization. These should be drawn from your backlog of potential product improvements or feature requests.

2. Estimate impact and effort

For each user story or theme, estimate the impact and effort involved. You can use quantitative metrics, qualitative assessments, or a combination of both. Consider factors such as user feedback, customer surveys, market research, and business goals to make these estimates as accurate as possible.

3. Plot on the matrix

Create a two-dimensional matrix or graph, with the X-axis representing effort (usually on a logarithmic scale) and the Y-axis representing impact. Place each user story or theme on the graph according to its estimated effort and impact.

- High Impact, Low Effort: These are quick wins that can provide significant value with minimal effort. Prioritize them as they offer a high return on investment.

- High Impact, High Effort: These are important but resource-intensive tasks. Evaluate their strategic importance and prioritize them accordingly, considering their long-term benefits.

- Low Impact, Low Effort: These may not be your top priorities, but they are relatively easy to implement. Consider them for inclusion if you have the capacity.

- Low Impact, High Effort: These are typically candidates for deprioritization, as they require substantial resources for limited gains. Reevaluate their relevance or consider them for the long term.

4. Make informed decisions.

Based on the positioning of user stories and themes on the matrix, you can now make informed decisions about prioritization. Focus your efforts on those in the high-impact zones, considering the balance between impact and effort. Keep in mind that while quick wins are valuable, long-term strategic goals are also essential for sustainable product growth.

Another common framework that has gained widespread recognition for its simplicity and effectiveness is MoSCoW. In this section, we'll explore the MoSCoW method, how it works, and why it's an invaluable tool for prioritizing user stories and themes.

MoSCoW Framework

The MoSCoW framework is an acronym that stands for:

- Must-have
- Should-have
- Could-have
- Won't-have

This framework categorizes user stories and features into these four distinct priority levels, helping product managers, development teams, and stakeholders align on what should be addressed in a given development cycle or release.

1. Must-Have (M)

Must-have items represent the core functionality or features that are non-negotiable for the success of your product or project. These are the essential elements that must be implemented in the current release to provide a minimum viable product (MVP) or to meet critical customer needs. Failure to deliver on these items could result in significant negative consequences, such as a product that is unusable or non-compliant with essential requirements.

Examples of Must-have items may include:

- User authentication for a new app

- A functioning shopping cart for an e-commerce website

- Core security features for a banking application

2. Should-Have (S)

Should-have items represent features or user stories that are important for the success of your product but are not as critical as Must-have items. These are the features that enhance the product's value, user experience, or market competitiveness. While not mandatory for a minimum viable product, they are highly desirable and should be prioritized after addressing Must-have items.

Examples of Should-have items may include:

- Social media sharing functionality in a content-sharing app

- Advanced search filters on an e-commerce platform

- Integration with third-party analytics tools for a marketing dashboard

3. Could-Have (C)

Could-have items are features or user stories that are nice to have but are not essential for the immediate release. These are typically lower-priority items that, if implemented, would provide additional value or convenience to users. However, they can be deferred to future releases or iterations without compromising the product's core functionality.

Examples of Could-have items may include:

- Personalized user profiles with customizable avatars

- Integration with a niche payment gateway for a broader customer base

- An optional dark mode theme for a mobile application

4. Won't-Have (W)

Won't-have items are those that are explicitly excluded from the current scope or release. These are features or user stories that have been considered and deliberately deprioritized due to factors such as time constraints, resource limitations, or a lack of alignment with current strategic goals. Won't-Have items are important to document to avoid scope creep and maintain focus on the essentials.

Examples of Won't-have items may include:

- Implementing cryptocurrency payments in a traditional banking app

- Developing a native mobile app for a web-based SaaS product

- Adding gamification elements to a productivity tool

Applying the MoSCoW Framework

To apply the MoSCoW framework effectively, follow these steps:

1. List User Stories and Features: Begin by listing all the user stories and features in your backlog.

2. Assign Priorities: Categorize each item into one of the four MoSCoW categories based on its importance and urgency. Be sure to involve relevant stakeholders, such as product owners, developers, and designers, in this process to ensure alignment.

3. Review and Refine: Regularly review and refine the priorities as the project progress and as new information becomes available. Adjustments may be necessary based on changing customer needs, market dynamics, or internal constraints.

Benefits of Using MoSCoW

The MoSCoW framework offers several benefits for product managers and development teams:

- Clarity: It provides a clear and structured way to communicate and align on priorities among team members and stakeholders.

- Focus: It helps maintain a focus on delivering essential functionality first, ensuring that critical user needs are addressed promptly.

- Flexibility: MoSCoW allows for flexibility in planning by

accommodating both core requirements and desirable enhancements.

- Scope Control: It helps prevent scope creep by explicitly defining what will not be included in the current release.

- Efficient Resource Allocation: By distinguishing between Must-have and Should-have items, it ensures that limited resources are allocated to the most critical tasks first.

Conclusion

The MoSCoW framework is a powerful and practical tool for prioritizing user stories and features in product development. It brings clarity, alignment, and structure to the prioritization process, helping teams make informed decisions about what to focus on in each development cycle or release. By leveraging MoSCoW, you can ensure that your product development efforts align with strategic objectives and deliver maximum value to your users and stakeholders.

Another valuable framework is the Kano Model. In this section, we'll explore the Kano Model, its principles, and how it can be applied to prioritize user stories and themes strategically.

Kano Model

The Kano Model, developed by Professor Noriaki Kano in the 1980s, is a powerful tool for understanding how different attributes or features of a product impact customer satisfaction. It categorizes these attributes into five distinct categories, each with a unique relationship to customer expectations and satisfaction.

1. Basic needs (must be quality)

Basic needs represent fundamental features that customers expect as a minimum requirement. When these features are absent or deficient, they lead to dissatisfaction, but their presence does not significantly increase satisfaction. Meeting basic needs is essential for customer retention and avoiding negative feedback.

Examples of Basic Needs:

- In a smartphone, the ability to make and receive calls without dropouts or errors

- In a web browser, fast and accurate rendering of web pages

2. Performance Needs (One-Dimensional Quality)

Performance needs are features where the relationship between performance and satisfaction is linear. In other words, the better you deliver on these attributes, the more satisfied customers will be. However, falling short of expectations doesn't necessarily lead to dissatisfaction; it just means missed opportunities for increased satisfaction.

Examples of Performance Needs:

- Battery life in a laptop: longer battery life generally leads to higher satisfaction.

- Speed and responsiveness of a website; faster load times contribute to greater satisfaction.

3. Excitement Needs (Attractive Quality)

Excitement needs are unexpected or delightful features that go beyond customer expectations. When these features are present, they lead to higher satisfaction and even delight. However, their absence doesn't necessarily cause dissatisfaction, as customers didn't initially expect them.

Examples of Excitement Needs:

- Voice-activated commands in a car's infotainment system

- Augmented reality filters in a photo editing app

4. Indifferent Needs (Indifferent Quality)

Indifferent needs represent attributes that don't significantly impact customer satisfaction, whether present or absent. Customers are generally indifferent to these features, and their inclusion doesn't drive satisfaction.

Examples of Indifferent Needs:

- A car's cup holder design

- The font used in an email client

5. Reverse Needs (Reverse Quality)

Reverse needs are features where the presence of a particular attribute leads to dissatisfaction, while its absence results in satisfaction. These features often represent customer preferences that contradict the product's design or purpose.

Examples of Reverse Needs:

- Overly complex menus and settings on a smartphone

- Intrusive pop-up ads in a mobile app

Applying the Kano Model for Prioritization

The Kano Model can be a powerful tool for prioritizing user stories and themes by aligning them with customer satisfaction categories. Here's how to apply it effectively:

1. Identify Customer Needs

Begin by understanding your customers' needs and expectations through surveys, interviews, and feedback analysis. Categorize these needs into the five Kano categories: basic, performance, excitement, indifferent, and reverse.

2. Map User Stories and Themes

Map your user stories and themes to the corresponding Kano categories based on how they address customer needs. This mapping helps you understand the impact of each item on customer satisfaction.

3. Prioritize Based on Category

Prioritize user stories and themes within each Kano category:

- Basic Needs: Ensure that all basic needs are met before focusing on other categories.

- Performance Needs: Prioritize features that can enhance the product's performance and align with customer expectations.

- Excitement Needs: Consider including some excitement needs to delight customers and create a competitive edge.

- Indifferent Needs: These can be deprioritized unless there are specific business or market reasons to address them.

- Reverse Needs: Avoid or mitigate features that fall into the Reverse Needs category to prevent dissatisfaction.

4. Monitor and Adapt

Continuously monitor customer satisfaction and feedback to ensure that your prioritization aligns with evolving customer expectations. As customer needs change, adjust your prioritization to meet those changing needs effectively.

Benefits of Using the Kano Model

The Kano Model offers several benefits for product managers and development teams:

- Customer-Centric Focus: It places customer satisfaction at the center of product development, ensuring that features align with customer expectations and needs.

- Strategic Prioritization: It helps prioritize features and improvements based on their impact on customer satisfaction and competitive advantage.

- Innovation Guidance: The Excitement Needs category encourages innovation and differentiation to exceed customer expectations.

- Preventing Dissatisfaction: It helps identify and mitigate features that could lead to customer dissatisfaction (reverse needs).

Conclusion

The Kano Model is a valuable framework for product managers seeking to prioritize user stories and themes while taking customer satisfaction into account. By categorizing features into Basic needs, Performance Needs, Excitement Needs, Indifferent

Value vs. Complexity Matrix

The Value vs. Complexity Matrix is a versatile tool that assists in this critical decision-making process. In this section, we'll explore the Value vs. Complexity Matrix, its principles, and how to apply it for prioritization.

It is a visual tool that categorizes user stories, features, or initiatives based on two primary dimensions:

1. Value

The value dimension represents the potential impact or benefit that a user story or theme can deliver. It assesses the feature's significance in terms of customer satisfaction, revenue generation, strategic alignment, or other relevant factors.

2. Complexity

The complexity dimension assesses the effort, resources, and technical intricacies required to implement the user story or theme successfully. It considers factors such as development time, technical expertise, potential risks, and dependencies.

By plotting user stories or themes on the Value vs. Complexity Matrix, you can gain insights into which items offer the most significant value relative to their implementation complexity.

Creating a Value vs. Complexity Matrix

To create and utilize a value vs. complexity matrix effectively, follow these steps:

1. Identify user stories or themes

Begin by listing the user stories or themes you want to evaluate for prioritization. These should be drawn from your backlog of potential product improvements or feature requests.

2. Estimate Value and Complexity

For each user story or theme, estimate the value it can provide to your product or business and the complexity involved in implementing it. Consider both quantitative and qualitative factors, such as customer feedback, market research, and strategic alignment.

3. Plot on the Matrix

Create a two-dimensional matrix or graph, with the X-axis representing complexity and the Y-axis representing value. Place each user story or theme on the graph according to its estimated value and complexity.

- High Value, Low Complexity: These are low-hanging fruits that offer significant benefits with minimal effort. Prioritize them as they provide a high return on investment.

- High Value, High Complexity: These are valuable but resource-intensive tasks. Evaluate their strategic importance and prioritize them accordingly, considering their long-term benefits.

- Low Value, Low Complexity: These may not be your top

priorities, but they are relatively easy to implement. Consider them for inclusion if you have the capacity.

- Low Value, High Complexity: These are typically candidates for deprioritization, as they require substantial resources for limited gains. Reevaluate their relevance or consider them for the long term.

4. Make Informed Decisions.

Based on the positioning of user stories and themes on the Value vs. Complexity Matrix, you can now make informed decisions about prioritization. Focus your efforts on those in the high-value zones, considering the balance between value and complexity. Keep in mind that while quick wins are valuable, long-term strategic goals are also essential for sustainable product growth.

Benefits of Using the Value vs. Complexity Matrix

The Value vs. Complexity Matrix offers several benefits for product managers and development teams:

- Clarity: It provides a clear and structured way to communicate and align on priorities among team members and stakeholders.

- Focus: It helps maintain a focus on delivering high-value functionality first, ensuring that critical user needs are addressed promptly.

- Efficiency: By distinguishing between high-value and low-value, low-complexity items, it optimizes resource allocation and development efforts.

- Risk Mitigation: It enables you to identify and manage high-complexity, low-value items that may pose risks to your project.

- Strategic Alignment: It ensures that your development efforts align with your product's strategic objectives and vision.

Conclusion

The Value vs. Complexity Matrix is a valuable tool for product managers seeking to prioritize user stories and themes effectively. By using this framework, you can make informed decisions that balance the potential value of features with their complexity to implement. This approach ultimately leads to a more competitive, customer-centric, and successful product.

RICE Framework

The RICE framework is a highly effective tool that helps you make data-driven decisions by considering the reach, impact, confidence, and effort of each potential feature or improvement. In this section, we'll delve into the RICE framework, how it works, and how to apply it for prioritization.

The RICE framework is an acronym that stands for:

- **Reach**

- **Impact**

- **Confidence**

- **Effort**

Each of these factors is assigned a numerical score to evaluate the potential value and feasibility of a user story or theme.

1. Reach

Reach assesses the number of users or customers who will be affected by the implementation of a user story or theme. It quantifies the scale of impact, measuring how widely the feature will be used or how many users it will benefit.

Reach is typically scored on a scale from 1 to 10, with 1 representing a small audience and 10 indicating a feature that would affect nearly all users.

2. Impact

Impact measures the potential business or user benefit that a user story or theme can deliver. It evaluates how significant the change or improvement will be in terms of customer satisfaction, revenue generation, or strategic alignment.

Impact is also scored on a scale from 1 to 10, with 1 representing minimal impact and 10 indicating a feature that could have a transformative effect.

3. Confidence

Confidence represents the level of certainty or confidence you have in your reach, impact, and effort estimates. It considers the quality of data, the reliability of assumptions, and the degree of uncertainty.

Confidence is typically scored as a percentage, ranging from 1% (low confidence) to 100% (high confidence).

4. Effort

Effort quantifies the resources, time, and complexity required to implement the user story or theme successfully. It considers factors such as development time, technical expertise, potential risks, and dependencies.

Effort is typically scored in person-months or person-weeks, depending on your team's preferred unit of measurement.

Calculating the RICE Score

To calculate the RICE score for a user story or theme, you use the following formula:

RICE SCORE = R x I X C / E

The resulting RICE score provides a numerical value that reflects the potential value and feasibility of the item. A higher RICE score indicates a more favorable prioritization.

Applying the RICE Framework for Prioritization

To apply the RICE framework effectively, follow these steps:

1. Identify User Stories or Themes
Start by listing the user stories or themes you want to evaluate for prioritization. These should be drawn from your backlog of potential product improvements or feature requests.

2. Estimate Reach, Impact, Confidence, and Effort

For each user story or theme, estimate the reach, impact, confidence, and effort values. This requires input from various stakeholders, including product managers, developers, designers, and data analysts. Ensure that the estimates are as accurate as possible.

3. Calculate the RICE Score

Apply the RICE formula to each user story or theme to calculate its RICE score. This score represents the priority of the item based on its potential impact, reach, confidence in estimates, and effort required.

4. Prioritize Based on RICE Scores

Prioritize user stories and themes based on their RICE scores, with higher scores indicating higher priority. Focus your development efforts on items with the highest RICE scores to maximize the potential impact and value delivered.

5. Monitor and Refine

Regularly monitor the progress and outcomes of the prioritized items. As new data becomes available, adjust your RICE scores and priorities accordingly to ensure that you continue to focus on the most valuable and feasible initiatives.

Benefits of Using the RICE Framework

The RICE framework offers several benefits for product managers and development teams:

- Data-Driven Decision-Making: It provides a structured, data-driven approach to prioritization, reducing reliance on subjective judgement.

- Focus on High-Impact Initiatives: It directs resources and effort towards user stories and themes with the potential for the greatest impact.

- Resource Optimization: By considering effort and feasibility, it helps allocate resources efficiently.

- Confidence Assessment: It encourages teams to evaluate and communicate the level of confidence in their estimates.

Conclusion

The RICE framework is a powerful tool for product managers seeking to prioritize user stories and themes based on data-driven criteria. By considering reach, impact, confidence, and effort, you can make informed decisions that lead to the development of high-impact features and improvements. This approach ultimately contributes to a more competitive, customer-centric, and successful product.

Practical Approach: Intercow uses the RICE framework for feature prioritization. They assess the reach (number of users affected), impact (expected improvement), confidence (certainty of the impact), and effort (development resources required) for each feature. This helps them make data-driven decisions on what to build.

Weighted Scoring

Weighted scoring, sometimes referred to as a scoring model or prioritization matrix, is a method that assigns numerical values to various factors or criteria associated with user stories and themes. These values are then used to calculate an overall score for each item, allowing for systematic prioritization based on predefined priorities.

The fundamental components of a weighted scoring model include:

1. Factors or Criteria

These are the attributes, characteristics, or dimensions you want to consider when prioritizing user stories and themes. Factors can vary significantly depending on your project and goals. Common factors include customer impact, strategic alignment, technical complexity, and business value.

2. Weightings

Each factor is assigned a weight or importance score relative to the other factors. These weights reflect the significance of each factor in the context of your project. Weightings are typically represented as percentages, with the total weightings adding up to 100%.

3. Scoring Method

A scoring method defines how you evaluate or rate each user story or theme for each factor. Scoring methods can be numerical (e.g., on a scale from 1 to 5), qualitative (e.g., high, medium, or low), or a combination of both.

4. Calculation of the Total Score

The total score for each user story or theme is calculated by multiplying the score for each factor by its respective weighting and summing these products. The result is a numerical value that represents the prioritization score for that item.

Applying weighted scoring for prioritization

To apply weighted scoring effectively, follow these steps:

1. Define Factors and Weightings

Start by identifying the factors or criteria that are relevant to your project and align them with your goals. Assign weight to each factor based on their relative importance. Ensure that the total weigh equal 100%.

2. Establish Scoring Guidelines

Define clear guidelines for scoring each factor. If using numerical ratings, specify the scale and what each score represents. If using qualitative ratings, provide descriptions or examples for each level (e.g., high, medium, or low).

3. Score User Stories and Themes

Evaluate each user story or theme based on the defined factors and weightings. Apply the scoring method to assign a score for each factor. Repeat this process for all items in your backlog.

4. Calculate Total Scores

Calculate the total score for each user story or theme by multiplying the factor scores by their respective weightings and summing these products. The result is an overall prioritization score for each item.

5. Prioritize Based on Total Scores

Sort the user stories and themes based on their total scores, with higher scores indicating higher priority. This ordered list serves as your prioritized backlog.

6. Periodic Review and Adjustment

Regularly review and adjust the weightings and scoring criteria as your project progresses, goals evolve, or new information becomes available. Weighted scoring should be a dynamic process that adapts to changing circumstances.

Benefits of Using Weighted Scoring

Weighted scoring offers several benefits for product managers and development teams:

- Customization: It allows you to tailor prioritization to the specific needs and objectives of your project.

- Objective Decision-Making: By quantifying factors and weightings, it reduces the influence of subjective biases in prioritization.

- Alignment with Strategy: It ensures that user stories and themes align with strategic goals and priorities.

- Clarity and Transparency: It provides a clear and transparent way to communicate priorities to team members and stakeholders.

For the image, write the reprioritization memo for internal communication.

Conclusion

Weighted scoring is a versatile and customizable approach to prioritizing user stories and themes in product management. By assigning importance to different factors and criteria, you can make informed decisions that align with your project's goals and objectives. This method ultimately contributes to the development of a more focused, strategic, and successful product.

Framework	When to use it	Key Strengths	Considerations
Kano Model	-Understanding customer satisfaction and delight. -Categorizing features into satisfaction categories	Categorizes features into five distinct categories: 1. **Basic Needs**: Identifies fundamental features that are expected and can cause dissatisfaction if missing. 2. **Performance Needs**: Assesses the linear relationship between performance and satisfaction. 3. **Excitement Needs**: Recognizes delightful, unexpected features that can significantly increase satisfaction. 4. **Indifferent Needs**: Identifies features that don't significantly impact satisfaction. 5. **Reverse Needs**: Flags features whose presence leads to dissatisfaction. Provides insights into basic needs, performance enhancers, or delighters.	-does not offer a quantitative assessment of potential value. -may require ongoing customer feedback to maintain relevance.
MoSCoW	-Establishing clear priorities. -Categorizing items	Provides straightforward categories for prioritization: **Must-Have**: Ensures critical features are addressed first. **Should-Have**:	-may not provide a structured scoring system like RICE.

	based on importance.	Identifies important features to enhance the product. **Could-Have**: Acknowledges features that are desirable but not critical. **Won't-Have**: Explicitly excludes features from the current scope; focuses on essential features first.	requires effective communication and alignment among team members and stakeholders.
RICE Framework	-Making data-driven decisions. -Quantifying potential value and feasibility.	Offers a systematic approach to prioritize based on data: **Reach**: Evaluates the number of users or customers affected by a feature. **Impact**: measures the potential business or user benefit. **Confidence**: Accounts for the level of certainty in estimates. **Effort**: Considers the resources and complexity required for implementation. - Focuses on high-impact, feasible initiatives.	-requires accurate data and estimates for reach, impact, confidence, and effort. -may necessitate ongoing data collection and analysis to maintain accuracy.
Value vs. Complexity Matrix	- Balancing value and complexity. -Assessing trade-offs between benefit and effort.	- Offers a visual representation of value versus complexity, aiding in decision-making. - **High Value, Low Complexity**: Quick wins with significant benefits - **High Value, High Complexity**: Strategic	- may not provide a structured scoring system like RICE. -requires clear definitions of value and

		initiatives with substantial benefits - **Low Value, Low Complexity**: Low-priority items that are easy to implement. - **Low Value, High Complexity**: Candidates for deprioritization due to effort versus benefit. Identifies quick wins and strategic initiatives.	complexity, which can be subjective.
Weighted Scoring	- Customization and alignment with project goals are essential.	- Allows for flexibility and customization: - Defines specific factors and criteria relevant to the project's objectives. - Assigns weightings to factors based on their relative importance. - Utilizes a scoring method to evaluate each factor for user stories or themes. - Prioritization with unique project needs and objectives.	- requires careful consideration of factors, weightings, and scoring methods, which can be time-consuming. - may require ongoing adjustments as project goals evolve.

Each framework offers a distinct approach to prioritization, and the choice of framework depends on your project's specific context, goals, and available data. Understanding the key strengths and considerations of each framework empowers you to make informed decisions and build a comprehensive toolkit for effective prioritization in the dynamic field of product management.

Iterate and Adapt

Remember that prioritization is not a one-time event but an ongoing process. As new information becomes available, customer needs evolve, and market conditions change, be prepared to revisit, and adjust your prioritization. Agile development encourages flexibility and adaptability, allowing you to fine-tune your product roadmap as needed.

5 IMPLEMENTATIONS

In the intricate and dynamic world of product management, the rubber meets the road during the execution phase of your product strategy. It's here that strategic vision and planning transform into tangible results. This chapter is your guide to effectively executing your product strategy, covering critical aspects from timing product releases to creating high-performing product teams.

Timing of product release

Timing product releases is a delicate art. It's not just about what you release; it's also about when and how you release it, which can make or break your product's success. In this section, we delve into the strategic considerations of timing your product releases, exploring two primary approaches:

1. Continuous and Incremental Updates: The Agile Cadence

Pros:

- Agile Responsiveness: This approach allows you to remain agile and responsive. You can swiftly adapt to user feedback and evolving market dynamics, implementing improvements as they become available.

- User Engagement: Users value consistent updates that cater to their needs. Regular releases keep them engaged and signal your unwavering commitment to enhancing their experience.

- Mitigated Risk: Smaller, incremental updates are generally less risky, as they are less likely to introduce major disruptions or issues to the user experience.

Cons:

- Flying Under the Radar: Continuous updates may not generate the same level of excitement or media attention as grand releases. Users may overlook smaller changes.

- Resource Intensiveness: Managing a continuous stream of updates demands ongoing resources from your team, which can be demanding.

2. Milestone Releases for Impact: The Grand Showcase

Pros:

- Creating a Buzz: Milestone releases offer the stage for creating a substantial buzz and attracting media coverage. They have the power to generate excitement and anticipation among both users and stakeholders.

- Narrative Clarity: Milestone releases enable you to craft a compelling narrative about your product's evolution. You can effectively spotlight major enhancements and thrilling new features.

- Focused Marketing: Marketing efforts can be concentrated on a single, monumental event, making it easier to reach a wide audience and gain attention.

Cons:

- Extended Timelines: Preparing for milestone releases

typically entails longer development and testing phases, which may postpone the delivery of valuable features to users.

- Heightened Risk: The complexity of milestone releases can introduce greater risks, including potential bugs or user disruptions if not meticulously tested.

- User Patience: Users might grow impatient if they must wait for significant updates, potentially leading to decreased engagement.

Choosing Your Strategic Approach

The choice between continuous updates and milestone releases hinges on several factors, each affecting your product's trajectory:

- Product Life Stage: In the early stages of a product's journey, continuous updates enable rapid iteration and feedback collection. As your product matures, milestone releases can be more fitting for creating market buzz.

- User Preferences: Grasp your users' inclinations and expectations. Some users relish frequent updates, while others await substantial, impactful releases.

- Market Dynamics: Keep an eye on your competitors and market trends. Sometimes, aligning with the trend of milestone releases might be essential for maintaining competitiveness.

- Resource Allocation: Evaluate your team's capabilities and resources. Continuous updates necessitate ongoing efforts, whereas milestone releases demand concentrated work over a specific timeframe.

- Strategic Goals: Ensure your release strategy aligns with your strategic objectives. Disrupting the market may warrant milestone releases, while preserving a loyal user base may favor a steady stream of continuous updates.

In essence, the choice isn't a one-size-fits-all proposition. Product managers should carefully evaluate these strategies within the context of their unique product, market, and user base. Strive to strike a harmonious balance between a consistent cadence of improvements and the grandeur of milestone releases to achieve sustained success.

Case Example: Finding the Right Tempo: A Story of Product Release Strategies

Meet ExpTech, a machine learning experiment tracking tool on a revolutionary MLOps platform named "SageTech". As the product manager of SageTech, Abhi is tasked with determining the optimal strategy for releasing new features and updates. SageTech has gained a considerable user base since its launch.

The ExpTech Dilemma

Abhi faces a common product management dilemma: how to time product releases effectively. She contemplates two distinct approaches—continuous and incremental updates versus milestone releases. The choice, she knows, will significantly impact user engagement, market perception, and the overall success of ExpTech.

Continuous and Incremental Updates: The Agile Approach

Pros:

- Agile Responsiveness: Abhi recognizes that ExpTech's users value timely improvements. He believes that a continuous update approach will allow his team to remain agile, promptly addressing user feedback and evolving market trends.

- User Engagement: Continuous updates would keep ExpTech users engaged, demonstrating the team's unwavering commitment to enhancing their MLOps journey.

Cons:

- Under the Radar: Abhi acknowledges that constant updates may not create the same level of excitement as major releases. Users might not notice smaller changes, and media coverage could be limited.

- Resource Intensiveness: Managing a stream of regular updates demands ongoing effort and resources, which SageTech's team might find taxing.

Milestone Releases for Impact: The Grand Showcase

Pros:

- Creating Buzz: Abhi knows that milestone releases offer the perfect stage for creating significant buzz. They can attract media attention and generate anticipation among users.

- Narrative Clarity: Abhi envisions crafting a compelling narrative around ExpTech's evolution. Major releases would allow him to spotlight substantial enhancements and thrilling new features.

Cons:
- Extended Timelines: Abhi recognizes that preparing for milestone releases would entail longer development and testing phases, potentially postponing the delivery of valuable features to users.

- Heightened Risk: Abhi is aware that the complexity of milestone releases could introduce greater risks, including potential bugs or user disruptions if not meticulously tested.

Abhi's Decision and Its Impact

After careful deliberation, Abhi opts for a balanced approach that combines both continuous updates and milestone releases. He reasons that this hybrid strategy allows ExpTech to maintain user engagement through regular improvements while also building excitement for significant feature releases.

- Continuous Updates: ExpTech continues to roll out regular

updates addressing user feedback and minor improvements, ensuring user engagement and satisfaction.

- Milestone Releases: Abhi schedules major milestone releases once every six months, introducing new features or substantial enhancements. These releases draw media attention and create a buzz among users.

Abhi's strategic decision yields impressive results. ExpTech enjoys a consistently engaged and satisfied user base due to continuous updates. Simultaneously, milestone releases garner attention from fitness enthusiasts and the media, resulting in a substantial increase in user acquisition and retention. Abhi's adept blend of both strategies enables SageTech to thrive and establish a strong presence in the competitive MLOps market.

In this case, Abhi underscores the importance of considering context, user expectations, and resource availability when choosing between product release strategies. His hybrid approach strikes the right balance and propels SageTech towards sustained success.

Choosing Milestone Names: The Art of Communication

The way you manage product milestones and version control can have a profound impact on the success of your product. It's not just about choosing names; it's about communicating the significance of each release, making iterative improvements, and maintaining order in your development process. Let's dive into the intricacies of this critical aspect.

The names you give to your product milestones are more than just labels; they're a means of communication. They convey the essence and significance of each release.

Here's how to go about it:

- Alignment with Strategy: Ensure that the name of each milestone aligns with your overall product strategy and the specific objectives you aim to accomplish with that release. It should tell a story of progress towards your strategic goals.

- Clarity and Simplicity: Keep the names clear, simple, and jargon-free. Your entire team, from developers to marketers, should easily understand what each milestone represents.

- User-Centric Approach: Consider naming milestones in a way that resonates with your target users. Make it relatable to their needs and expectations, reinforcing the value they can expect.

- Collective Decision-Making: Involve your product team in the naming process. It's a collaborative effort where designers, developers, marketers, and other stakeholders can collectively decide on names that encapsulate the essence of each milestone.

- Periodic Review: Milestone names aren't set in stone. They should evolve with your product. Periodically review them to ensure they still accurately reflect your product's direction. Don't hesitate to rename milestones if they no longer align with your current objectives.

Adding a "Plus" Version: Incremental Enhancements

The introduction of a "Plus" version or an iterative release can signal incremental improvements or added features. Here's what to consider:

- Significance of Enhancements: A "plus" version should represent more than just minor tweaks. It should signify substantial improvements or additions that warrant a separate release.

- User Benefit: Ensure that the "Plus" version brings tangible benefits to users. Whether it's enhanced functionality, improved performance, or additional features, users should perceive real value.

- Effective Communication: Clearly communicate the value and significance of the "Plus" version to your users and stakeholders. Make it evident why this release deserves their attention.

- Iterative vs. Overhaul: Assess whether the changes are iterative improvements to an existing version or a significant overhaul. The "Plus" designation should align with the magnitude of the enhancements.

Leveraging Version Control: Maintaining Order

Version control is the compass that guides your product development journey. Here's how to make the most of it:

- Semantic Versioning: Embrace semantic versioning (e.g., MAJOR.MINOR.PATCH) to convey the importance of each release. It's a language developers and users understand major changes, minor additions, and bug fixes.

- Structured Branching: Implement a well-defined branching strategy in your version control system. This helps manage parallel development efforts, track features, and address bug fixes more efficiently.

- Detailed Release Notes: Document comprehensive release notes for each version. These notes should outline changes, improvements, and any potential impact on users. Transparency fosters trust.

- Rollback Planning: Plan for contingencies. Develop a rollback strategy in case issues arise post-release. Being prepared to revert to a stable version ensures you can address unforeseen challenges swiftly.

- Collaborative Effort: Promote collaboration between your development and quality assurance teams. This ensures that code changes are tracked, tested, and validated before each release.

User-Centric Decision Making

Above all, let user needs and preferences guide your decision-making. Prioritize enhancements and releases that align with user expectations and provide real value. Solicit feedback, analyze user data, and be agile in adapting your approach based on user insights.

Effective milestone management and version control aren't just about maintaining order; they're about delivering value consistently to your users with each release. By carefully considering these aspects, you not only navigate product milestones and version control effectively but also enhance your product's overall journey towards success.

Assigning Ownership and Responsibilities

In the world of product management, one of the foundational elements for success is the careful assignment of roles and responsibilities. It's like assembling a well-coordinated team for an exciting mission. This section delves into the critical art of effectively assigning ownership and responsibilities.

Meet Your Team: Recognizing the Key Players

Imagine your product roadmap as a dynamic production. Before the show begins, it's essential to introduce your cast of characters. These individuals hail from various corners of your organization:

- Product Managers: They shape the overarching vision and strategy of the product.

- Developers: Developers are the builders who transform ideas into tangible features.

- Designers: The creative minds behind the user experience and aesthetics.

- Quality Assurance (QA) Teams: The guardians of product quality and reliability.

- Marketers: Marketers are the storytellers who convey your product's value.

- Customer Support: The troubleshooters who assist users and gather feedback.

- Sales Teams: The advocates who spread the word about your

product.

- Executives and Leadership: The compass that provides strategic direction and resources.

Who's in Charge: Clear and Accountable Roles

Now that you've introduced your cast, it's time to assign roles and responsibilities. Each element of your product roadmap should have a dedicated owner who takes responsibility for its success. This alignment ensures that everyone knows their part in the production. Here's how it's done:

- Choosing Dedicated Owners: Carefully select individuals or teams responsible for each milestone or feature in your roadmap. Ensure that ownership is unmistakable.

- Metrics that Matter: Define key performance indicators (KPIs) and metrics that owners should monitor. These metrics serve as the benchmarks for success.

- Smooth Handovers: Clarify when ownership transitions from one stage of development to another. Define the handover points clearly.

- Open Communication: Ownership goes beyond a mere title; it's a commitment. Ensure that owners understand expectations and maintain regular communication regarding progress.

What's My Role: Understanding Contributions

To create a well-coordinated team, it's crucial for each team member to comprehend their role and its contribution to the bigger picture. Clarity prevents confusion and empowers individuals to make meaningful contributions. Here's how it's achieved:

- Role Definitions: Provide clear definitions for each role within your product team. What does a product manager do compared to a developer or a designer? Establish clarity.

- Responsibilities on the Map: Clearly outline the specific responsibilities associated with each role in the context of the product roadmap. This includes tasks, decision-making authority, and collaboration expectations.

- Cross-Team Awareness: Encourage team members to gain an understanding of their colleagues' roles in other departments. This cultivates empathy and supports cross-functional collaboration.

- Regular Check-Ins: Host regular meetings or discussions to review roles and responsibilities. These gatherings offer an opportunity for team members to align and clarify any questions or concerns.

Let's Work Together: Collaboration and Communication

In the production of product development, different teams and departments must perform in harmony. Cross-functional collaboration is like the conductor's baton that keeps everyone synchronized. Here's how it's fostered:

- Tools for Collaboration: Utilize collaboration tools and platforms that facilitate seamless communication and knowledge sharing among teams.

- Team Gatherings: Organize regular cross-functional meetings to discuss progress, challenges, and opportunities. These gatherings promote transparency and open dialogue.

- Shared Goals: Ensure that all teams share a common understanding of the overarching objectives of your product roadmap. A shared vision naturally fosters collaboration.

- Feedback Exchange: Establish feedback mechanisms between teams to facilitate the exchange of insights and ideas for improvement.

Assigning ownership and responsibilities is not just a matter of logistics; it's about creating a culture where individuals work together with enthusiasm and accountability. By identifying your key players, aligning ownership, defining responsibilities, and promoting cross-functional collaboration, you establish an effective and cooperative environment for your product development journey.

Significance of Weekly Business Reviews

Staying on course and achieving your objectives requires a well-structured approach. Weekly Business Reviews (WBRs) are an integral part of this journey, serving as the compass that keeps you headed in the right direction. Let's explore why these regular check-ins are essential:

Alignment and focus.

Imagine WBRs as the North Star that keeps your team oriented. By revisiting your goals, tracking your progress, and discussing challenges weekly, WBRs ensure that everyone remains aligned with the broader strategic objectives. This alignment is the foundation of a cohesive and effective team.

Real-time problem solving

In the unpredictable landscape of product management, issues can arise at any moment. WBRs provide a dedicated platform for immediate discussions and collaborative problem-solving. This agility empowers your team to address challenges promptly, preventing them from growing into substantial obstacles.

Data-Driven decision making

Data is the currency of modern business. WBRs leverage data analysis to facilitate informed decision-making. This data-driven approach enables your team to make choices grounded in real-time information, enhancing the accuracy and effectiveness of your strategies.

Accountability

Regular reviews create a sense of accountability within your team.

Knowing that they will report on their progress motivates team members to fulfil their commitments. This culture of accountability fosters a results-oriented mindset, driving productivity and achievement.

Course correction

In a constantly evolving business environment, adaptability is paramount. WBRs allow your team to assess strategies regularly and make necessary adjustments. This agility ensures that your organization remains competitive and responsive to market dynamics.

Communication

Effective communication is the lifeblood of any organization. WBRs facilitate transparent and open communication between teams and leadership. This transparency builds trust and ensures that vital information flows freely throughout your organization.

Continuous improvement

WBRs cultivate a culture of continuous improvement. By identifying areas for enhancement and setting improvement goals, your team can refine their processes and approaches over time. This focus on improvement leads to greater efficiency and effectiveness.

Resource optimization

Resources are finite, including time, money, and personnel. WBRs enable your organization to allocate resources more efficiently by identifying areas where they can be best utilized and where adjustments are needed.

Employee engagement

Regular interaction through WBRs keeps employees engaged and invested in your organization's success. It provides a platform for them to voice concerns, share ideas, and feel that their contributions are valued.

Proactive risk management

By regularly reviewing performance and potential risks, WBRs enable your organization to proactively identify and mitigate issues before they escalate. This risk management approach reduces the likelihood of crises.

Goal achievement

WBRs serve as a progress tracker for your goals and objectives. When your team witnesses tangible progress and achievements, it boosts morale and motivation, propelling them to work harder towards accomplishing their targets.

Time savings

Contrary to the perception that WBRs consume time, they often save time in the long run. By addressing issues promptly, your team can prevent minor problems from escalating into major disruptions that require extensive time and effort to resolve.

In summary, within the realm of product management, WBRs are your guiding light on the path to success. They foster alignment, accountability, data-driven decision-making, and a culture of continuous improvement. By dedicating time and effort to WBRs, your organization can navigate challenges, optimize resources, and seize opportunities effectively, ensuring a successful product journey.

WBR Format

The below template can be customized to suit the specific needs and goals of the review:

Weekly Business Review
Date: [Insert Date] Time: [Insert Time] Location: [Insert Location or Virtual Meeting Link]
Meeting Agenda:

1. Opening Remarks (5 minutes)
   - Welcome and introductions.
   - Purpose of the review.

2. Review of Previous Week's Goals (10 minutes)
   - Recap the goals set in the last review.
   - Discuss progress made on each goal.

3. Key Metrics and Performance (15 minutes)
   - Present and analyze key performance indicators (KPIs).
   - Identify trends and areas of concern.
   - Celebrate achievements.

4. Market and Competitive Analysis (10 minutes)
   - Overview of the current market landscape.
   - Updates on competitors' activities and strategies.
   - Implications for our business.

5. Customer Insights (15 minutes)
   - Customer feedback and reviews.
   - Highlight any significant customer trends or issues.
   - Discuss actions taken in response to customer feedback.

6. Product and Service Updates (15 minutes)
   - Updates on product development and releases.
   - Service improvements or changes.
   - Future product roadmap.

7. Sales and Revenue (10 minutes)
   - Sales figures and revenue analysis.
   - Sales performance by product or category.
   - Discussion of any pricing changes or promotions.

8. Operational Updates (10 minutes)
   - Supply chain and inventory status.
   - Operational challenges and solutions.
   - Any upcoming logistical changes.

9. Marketing and Advertising (10 minutes)
   - Marketing campaign results.

- Advertising spends and ROI.
- Marketing plans for the upcoming week.

10. Team Reports and Action Items (15 minutes)
    - Reports from individual team members or departments.
    - Discussion of action items for the upcoming week.
    - Assign responsibilities and deadlines.

11. Wrap-up and Next Steps (5 minutes)
    - Summary of key takeaways.
    - Next week's goals and focus areas.
    - Any additional questions or comments.

12. Closing Remarks (5 minutes)
    - Thank you and acknowledgment of the team's efforts.
    - Reminder of the importance of the weekly review.

Meeting Participants:
- [List of Attendees]

Prepared by: [Your Name] Meeting facilitator: [Facilitator's Name] Meeting recorder: [Recorder's Name]

The above template provides a structured framework for a weekly business review meeting, allowing participants to track progress, discuss challenges, and plan effectively. Adapt it as needed to fit the specific requirements of your organization and the nature of the business being reviewed.

In the fast-paced realm of software development, the only constant is change. The relentless march of technology, evolving customer expectations, and unpredictable market shifts demand a development approach that can adapt and excel in an ever-shifting landscape. Agile methodologies, championed by the Scrum framework, have emerged as a powerful response to these challenges. In this chapter, we will dive deep into the essence of Agile principles and the Scrum framework, exploring how they empower product managers to lead successful projects with real-world examples.

The Foundation of Agile Software Development

Agile principles stand as the bedrock of contemporary software development, representing a profound shift from traditional project management to a dynamic, customer-centric approach. At the core of Agile lies the belief that collaboration, adaptability, and customer feedback are essential to crafting high-quality software products. This paradigm shift has reshaped how teams conceptualize, plan, and execute projects.

The Agile Ensemble

Central to Agile is the concept of the "Agile Ensemble," a set of practices and ceremonies that collectively ensure an organized and collaborative development process. Let's examine these components with real-life examples:

1. The Product Backlog: Imagine you're developing a mobile app. Your product backlog contains a diverse array of items, such as user stories and bug fixes. Suppose you receive user feedback requesting a new feature-the ability to share content with friends. You add this request to the product backlog, ensuring it's on your radar for future sprints.

2. The Sprint Backlog: During a sprint planning meeting, you select a subset of items from the product backlog for the upcoming two-week sprint. In this sprint, you choose to focus on enhancing the app's performance and implementing the 'share with friends' feature. This dynamic list of tasks becomes your sprint backlog.

3. Daily Stand-up Meetings: Every day, your development team gathers for a brief stand-up meeting. John, one of the developers, mentions that he's encountered a roadblock in implementing the 'share with friends' feature. The team discusses the issue and decides to pair-program to address it. This daily check-in keeps everyone aligned and ensures swift issue resolution.

Key Roles in Agile

The success of Agile teams' hinges on the roles they play. Let's look at these roles through real-world lenses:

1. Scrum Master: Think of the Scrum Master as the team's coach. Suppose your team encounters conflicts during a sprint. The Scrum Master steps in to facilitate conversations, mediate disputes, and ensure everyone remains focused on the sprint's goals. Their role is akin to that of a referee who ensures fair play.

2. Product Owner: In your mobile app project, the product owner serves as a bridge between your development team and the app's end-users. They actively gather feedback, conduct user surveys, and prioritize features based on user needs. For instance, after analyzing user feedback, they prioritize the 'share with friends' feature because it aligns with users' desires.

3. Development Team: Your development team comprises individuals with diverse skill sets, from app developers to UX designers. They self-organize to achieve the sprint goals, much like a well-coordinated orchestra where each musician plays a unique part, contributing to the symphony.

Agile Adaptability

One of Agile's hallmarks is its adaptability. Agile teams can nimbly adjust their course in response to changing requirements, customer feedback, and market dynamics. To illustrate, consider your mobile app project. Midway through a sprint, user surveys reveal that users prefer a different sharing mechanism than initially planned. Agile allows you to pivot swiftly, modifying your sprint backlog to accommodate this change and deliver what users truly want.

Continuous Improvement and Alignment

Agile processes incorporate ceremonies like the demo and review and the retrospective, which promote continuous improvement. These ceremonies ensure the team's practices align with the project's objectives and customer needs. For instance, after a sprint, your team holds a retrospective. You discuss what went well, such as the smooth integration of the 'share with friends' feature, and areas for improvement, like streamlining the testing process for future sprints.

User-Centric Design

User-centric design is a pivotal Agile principle, led by the product owner. Consider your app project: the product owner continually seeks user feedback and refines the 'share with friends' feature based on this input. This iterative approach results in a user-friendly and highly functional feature that resonates with the app's audience.

Conclusion

Agile methodologies and the Scrum framework prioritize adaptability, quality, transparency, and continuous integration, all while embracing real-world changes and customer feedback. In the dynamic world of software development, these principles are not just a choice; they are a necessity for those who aim to thrive in the competitive landscape. By following Agile's tenets and leveraging the Scrum framework, product managers can navigate the ever-changing terrain of software development with finesse, delivering products that truly delight their users.

Practical Approach: Take, for example, Spootify's use of Agile. They employ the Scrum framework for sprint planning, conduct daily stand-up meetings using Kanban boards, and focus on lean principles to eliminate waste. This combination allows them to deliver high-quality features and adapt to market changes swiftly.

First, congratulations on getting your software product to the final stages. But remember, even the greatest product needs a well-thought-out plan to make its mark. So, let's talk about how to get your software out there and tell people why it's awesome. In this section, we'll explore the important steps in launch planning and marketing, and we'll use some real-life examples to make things clear.

The Launch Plan: Making a Roadmap

Imagine your software as a car. To get it on the road and driving smoothly, you need a roadmap -a plan for what to do before the big launch day. Let's break down some of the key elements of this roadmap and look at examples:

1. Know Your Audience:

Before you hit the road, you need to know who's going along for the ride. If you've got project management software, think about the project managers, teams, and businesses who need it most.

2. Webinars:

Webinars are like virtual show-and-tell sessions. You can use them to demonstrate how your software works and how it can solve real problems. Let's say you're launching project management software. You could run webinars showing how it makes project management a breeze.

3. Content Marketing:

Blog posts, articles, and other written stuff can help people understand your software better. If you're releasing cybersecurity software, you might write blog posts about the latest security threats and how your software can protect people from them.

4. Emails:

Think of building an email list like gathering a group of excited friends for a road trip. You send them messages to get them hyped up. Leading up to your launch, send emails that give sneak peeks, updates, and exclusive information. It's like counting down the days until your trip.

5. Social Media Teasers:

Social media is your megaphone. Share short videos, sneak peeks, and behind-the-scenes stuff to get people talking. If you're launching cybersecurity software, post videos showing how your software can beat hackers at their own game.

6. Beta Testing:

Think of beta testing as a test drive. Get some early users to try your software and give feedback. It's like letting a few trusted friends take your car for a spin before the big road trip.

The Marketing Strategy: Making People Want to Join the Journey

Marketing is like telling everyone how amazing your road trip is going to be. It's about getting people excited before, during, and after the launch. Let's look at how to make it happen, with some real-world examples:

1.   Influencer Partnerships:

Think of influencers as your cool friends who tell everyone about your road trip. If you're launching a fitness app, partner with fitness trainers or health gurus who can tell their followers why your app is a game-changer.

2.   Paid Advertising:

Paid ads are like road signs pointing the way. Use them on Google or social media to make sure the right people see your message. If you're launching a language learning app, use ads that pop up when people search for language learning stuff.

3.   User Reviews and Testimonials:

Reviews and testimonials are like word-of-mouth recommendations from your friends. Get your early users to say good things about your software and share these on your website and in your ads. If you have a productivity tool, show how it helped people get more done.

4.   Community Building:

Building a community is like creating a club for people who love your product. If you're releasing video editing software, give users a place to share their creations, ask questions, and show off their skills.

5. Continuous Content Creation:

Content creation is like giving your road trip buddies interesting stories along the way. If you're releasing design software, keep creating tutorials, tips, and design inspiration to keep your users engaged and coming back for more.

6. Feedback Loops:

Staying in touch with your users is like asking your friends how the road trip is going and what they'd like to do next. If you have project management software, keep the conversation going to make sure you're giving users what they need.

Conclusion

In the world of software product management, launching and marketing are as important as the product itself. To make sure your product gets the attention it deserves, you need a plan and a strategy. So, put in the effort, adapt to what people are saying, and watch your software take off like the awesome journey it is. Remember, it's all about getting people excited about the road ahead.

Explain the image as part of product management.

Beta Testing: Transforming Early Users into Your Software's Champions

Beta testing is like having a group of eager friends over to your house to taste your delicious homemade lasagna before serving it at a big family gathering. It's not just a marketing strategy; it's a golden opportunity to refine your software and gather early user insights. In this section, we'll take a closer look at the different types of beta testing-private beta, public beta, and preview releases-and explore how and why to use them strategically. We'll also dive into the planning required to attract eager testers, discuss pricing strategies, and emphasize the role of beta testers in generating valuable testimonials.

Types of Beta Testing

1. Private Beta Testing: A Select Gathering

Think of this as hosting an intimate dinner party with close friends and family. You handpick a select group of testers, often including developers, friends, and family, who receive early access to your software. These testers provide valuable feedback without exposing your software to a wide audience.

Why Use Private Beta Testing?

- Controlled Environment: Private beta testing allows for meticulous testing in a controlled setting.
- Critical Issue Identification: Early testers can uncover significant problems before they reach a larger audience.
- Quality Enhancement: Insights from this group help fine-tune your software, ensuring a high-quality product.

Attracting Private Beta Testers:

- Reach out to your personal and professional network to find trusted testers.
- Utilize social media, forums, and developer communities to identify potential testers.
- Offer exclusive access or incentives to encourage

participation.

2. Public Beta Testing: Welcoming Everyone In

Imagine your home turned into an open house where everyone is invited. In public beta testing, a broader range of users gets a sneak peek at your software. This phase serves to uncover issues that may not surface during private beta, thanks to the diversity in devices, configurations, and usage patterns.

Why Use Public Beta Testing?

- Diverse Feedback: A larger pool of testers offers a wide array of insights and feedback.
- Stress Testing: Different devices and setups reveal how your software performs under real-world conditions.
- • Market Buzz: Public beta generates excitement and builds anticipation for your software's official release.

Attracting Public Beta Testers:

- Promote your public beta through your website, app stores, and social media platforms.
- Provide a sneak peek of your software's features and the benefits of joining the beta test.
- Encourage users to share their thoughts and feedback through in-app mechanisms.

3. Preview Releases: Offering a Glimpse of the Magic

Picture this as a movie trailer that teases the main event. In a preview release, a limited version of your software becomes available to the public, often with some features locked. It's all about creating excitement and curiosity before the grand unveiling.

Why Use Preview Releases?

- Building Anticipation: Preview releases create buzz and make people eager for the full software release.
- Attracting Early Adopters: You gain early users who provide

invaluable insights and feedback.
- Market Testing: This is a way to test the waters and assess how well your software fits within the market.

Attracting Users to Preview Releases:

- Offer a limited number of free preview versions to pique interest.
- Share the news through press releases and social media to generate buzz.
- Encourage users to provide feedback and even become advocates for your software.

Beta Testing, Planning, and Pricing Strategies

Attracting Beta Testers:

- Create a dedicated signup page on your website, making it easy for interested testers to join.
- Use targeted emails to reach out to potential testers.
- Promote your beta test on social media channels to inform and attract potential testers.
- Sweeten the deal with incentives like early access, exclusive features, or discounts on the final product.

Pricing During Beta:

- Decide whether you'll offer the beta version for free or at a reduced price.
- Be transparent about the temporary nature of beta pricing.
- Consider a freemium model, offering some features for free and reserving premium features for a cost.

Testimonials and Feedback:

- Actively seek feedback from beta testers and encourage them to share their experiences.
- Invite beta testers to provide testimonials about your software and participate in case studies.
- Showcase positive feedback and testimonials on your website

and in your marketing materials.

Conclusion

Beta testing is more than just finding and fixing bugs; it's an exciting phase of building your software and engaging with your earliest fans. Whether you opt for private, public, or preview beta testing, use this opportunity to refine your software and turn your testers into your most vocal supporters. Their insights can be invaluable in making your software truly exceptional, and their testimonials will serve as potent endorsements in your marketing efforts. Get ready for a thrilling journey, and let your testers be the heroes of your software's adventure.

Practical Approach: Drobpox's success is a classic example. They began with a simple video explaining their product, built a Minimum Viable Product (MVP), measured its usage and user feedback, and continuously learned and improved the product. This lean approach helped them grow into a billion-dollar company.

Business Case: Leveraging Beta Testing for Software Success

In the world of software development, the role of a product manager is akin to steering a ship through turbulent waters. The decisions made along the way can determine whether the product succeeds or sinks. In this business case, we explore the strategic decision-making process of a product manager regarding the implementation of beta testing for a new software product.

Our company, TechGenius, is on the verge of launching an innovative productivity software application called "WorkFlowPro." This software has the potential to be a game-changer in the market, but the product manager, Sarah, recognizes the importance of ironing out any issues before the official release.

Problem Statement

The primary challenge Sarah faces is ensuring that WorkFlowPro is well-received, free from major glitches, and capable of standing out in a competitive market. To address these concerns, Sarah is contemplating the adoption of a beta testing strategy.

Objectives

1. Quality Assurance: Ensure that WorkFlowPro is free from critical issues and glitches.

2. Diverse User Feedback: Gather insights from a diverse set of users to identify potential improvements.

3. Market Buzz: Generate excitement and anticipation for WorkFlowPro's official release.

Proposed Solution

Sarah's proposal is to implement beta testing through three phases: private beta, public beta, and preview releases, each serving distinct purposes.

1. Private Beta Testing:

    -   This initial phase will involve a select group of trusted testers, including developers and internal team members.

    -   The objective is to catch critical issues, ensure controlled testing, and fine-tune the software for a broader audience.

    -   Attracting private beta testers will involve outreach to personal and professional networks, with incentives like exclusive early access.

2. Public Beta Testing:

    -   The second phase will open the testing pool to a larger audience.

    -   The goal is to obtain diverse feedback, stress test the software, and generate market excitement.

    -   Attracting public beta testers will involve promotional efforts through the company's website, app stores, and social media platforms.

3. Preview Releases:

    -   The final phase will offer a limited version of WorkFlowPro to the public, providing a sneak peek with some features locked.

    -   This phase aims to build anticipation, attract early adopters, and assess market reception.

    -   Attracting users to preview releases will involve offering a limited number of free versions, generating buzz through press releases, and encouraging users to provide feedback and become advocates for the software.

Benefits

- Quality Improvement: Beta testing will allow the team to identify and address critical issues, leading to a higher-quality product.

- Diverse Insights: The diverse pool of beta testers will provide valuable feedback and insights from various perspectives.

- Market Anticipation: Beta testing will generate excitement and anticipation, creating a buzz in the market.

Risks and Mitigations

- Data Security: The exposure of a limited version of the software to the public during the preview phase carries potential security risks. Mitigation involves stringent data protection measures.

- Time Constraints: Beta testing may extend the product launch timeline. To address this, a clear timeline and deadline will be set for each beta testing phase.

Budget

The budget allocation for beta testing includes incentives for private beta testers, marketing costs for public beta testing, and promotional expenses for preview releases. The budget is estimated at $50,000.

In a competitive software market, the decision to implement a comprehensive beta testing strategy is vital. The proposed private beta, public beta, and preview release phases will not only ensure that WorkFlowPro is of the highest quality but will also generate excitement and anticipation among potential users. By addressing these objectives and risks systematically, we set the stage for a successful software launch, ultimately maximizing ROI and user satisfaction.

Post-Launch Monitoring

Imagine you've launched your software product into a bustling market. It's like sending your child off to college. You can't just let it go and forget about it. Post-launch monitoring is the way you keep an eye on your 'child,' ensuring it not only survives but thrives in the dynamic world out there. It's your continuous involvement, much like the regular calls and visits you have with your child during their college journey.

Choosing the Right Metrics and KPIs

Selecting the right metrics and KPIs is like ensuring you have the right tools in your toolbox. You wouldn't bring a lawnmower to a kitchen remodel, right? Similarly, KPIs act as specific tools needed to gauge your software's success. They are comparable to selecting the correct wrench for a plumbing job or using a measuring tape for carpentry. The key is to choose the ones that align with your product's goals and your users' needs. For example, metrics like Weekly Active Users (WAU), Monthly Active Users (MAU), and Month-over-Month (MoM) growth can serve as KPIs, helping you track user engagement and the software's performance.

Understanding User Engagement

User engagement functions as the heartbeat of your software. It's the enthusiasm and energy users bring to your product. Think of it as a friendly conversation with peers and acquaintances. The objective is to understand their experiences, identify what they enjoy, and discover areas for improvement. It's akin to sitting down with your friends, asking them about their day, and learning about their needs and expectations.

Technical Performance and Market Response

Just as a car's engine needs regular check-ups to ensure it runs smoothly, your software requires ongoing evaluation of its technical performance. This means closely monitoring aspects like load times, system crashes, and user experience. For instance, if you notice a sudden increase in loading times or frequent crashes, it's like identifying an unusual noise in your car's engine. Addressing these issues promptly is crucial to maintaining the software's reliability and providing a seamless experience to users.

Technical performance metrics include factors like server response times, error rates, and database efficiency. These metrics help in pinpointing areas that might need improvement, much like a mechanic identifying the source of a car's performance issues. It's all about ensuring your software runs like a well-maintained vehicle, delivering a smooth and trouble-free ride for users.

Just as a business keeps an eye on market trends and competitors, software products must closely monitor how the market responds and what the competition is up to. Market response is akin to understanding whether people prefer your product over others. For instance, if you observe a sudden drop in new users or growing interest in a competitor's software, it's like recognizing shifts in consumer preferences.

Analyzing market response involves tracking user adoption rates, customer reviews, and market share. This data helps in understanding the software's position in the market and whether changes are needed to stay competitive. It's like a business studying sales figures and customer feedback to adapt to evolving market dynamics. In the ever-evolving software world, keeping an eye on the competition and being responsive to market changes is vital to ensuring your product's success.

Customer Support and Product Updates

Think of delivering responsive customer support like offering top-notch service in a restaurant. When customers have questions or run into problems, they want a helpful and prompt response. It's akin to having attentive waitstaff who ensure that diners have a great experience.

Responsive customer support includes giving users multiple ways to reach out, such as through chat, email, or a helpdesk. This is like offering various methods for customers to get in touch with restaurant staff, like calling or emailing. The key is to provide quick and useful assistance, much like ensuring restaurant guests have a smooth and enjoyable meal.

Managing issue resolution and updates is like refining a restaurant menu to keep it fresh and appealing. Issue resolution means addressing and solving problems users encounter, much like adjusting a dish that didn't meet diners' expectations. Regular updates are akin to introducing new items or enhancing existing ones to create a better dining experience, just as restaurants tweak their menus to cater to changing tastes.

The secret to success lies in finding a balance between responsive customer support and a commitment to issue resolution and frequent updates. This balance ensures users are happy and the software remains competitive in an ever-changing landscape.

Data Security, Feedback Loops, and Reporting

In the digital world, data security and privacy compliance are as vital as safeguarding your home. Just as you lock your doors and windows, your software needs strong security measures to protect sensitive user data. This is akin to ensuring your home's security system is up to date.

Data breaches are like break-ins, with the potential to harm users and tarnish your software's reputation. To avoid such incidents, you need to implement robust security measures, including encryption, access controls, and regular security audits. This is like having a reliable alarm system, sturdy locks, and security cameras to protect your home from intruders.

Ensuring privacy compliance is like respecting your neighbor's boundaries. It involves following legal regulations and obtaining user consent for data collection and processing. Just as you wouldn't want your neighbor peering through your windows, users should feel confident that their data is handled with care and respect.

Feedback loops are the lifeblood of product improvement. Just as a skilled chef relies on customer feedback to refine dishes, your software benefits from feedback to enhance its features and user experience. Establishing collaborative feedback loops is like inviting patrons into the kitchen to provide input on menu changes.

Creating channels for user feedback, such as surveys, support tickets, or community forums, allows users to voice their concerns and suggestions. Much like a restaurant that encourages diners to share their experiences and preferences, this input guides product managers and developers in making informed decisions to meet user needs.

Effective reporting and communication are like the transparent windows in a restaurant's kitchen. They offer a view into what's happening behind the scenes. Similarly, in the software realm, transparent reporting and communication are crucial for building trust with users and stakeholders.

Regularly sharing insights gained from data, user feedback, and performance metrics is essential. Just as a restaurant may have an open kitchen policy to show how dishes are prepared, these reports offer a glimpse into the software's performance, user satisfaction, and areas for improvement. Effective communication fosters trust and shows users that their concerns and feedback are valued, much like a restaurant that listens to diners' comments and acts on them.

The combination of robust data security, open feedback loops, and transparent reporting creates a strong foundation for maintaining user trust and enhancing the software's quality.

6 COMMUNICATIONS

Imagine a product manager as the guiding force in a multifaceted, collaborative effort, much like a quarterback on the football field. In this endeavor, effective communication serves as the playbook that directs your team and product forward.

In the world of software and product development, having brilliant ideas isn't enough; you must convey them, align diverse individuals, and establish connections to transform those ideas into reality. Product managers wear multiple hats, functioning as not only tech-savvy individuals but also as skilled storytellers, diplomats, and team players. This chapter is dedicated to unveiling the pivotal role of communication in the dynamic world of product management.

We'll explore how to engage with a variety of stakeholders, from team members to executives, ensuring everyone understands and works towards the same goal. We'll also dive into the details of working closely with different departments, addressing challenging conversations with diplomacy, and highlighting why meticulous record-keeping is indispensable. Join us as we delve into the art of effective communication in the ever-evolving landscape of product management.

The Role of Communication in Product Management

Effective communication is not just a crucial aspect but the very essence of successful product management. It's the compass that guides every step in the product journey.

Understanding the Pivotal Role of Communication in Product Management

Consider the success of Apple's product launches. The pivotal role of communication is evident in how Apple conveys not just the features of their products, but also the experience and lifestyle they offer. It's not just about the technology; it's about effectively communicating how that technology fits into users' lives.

Just as Apple carefully orchestrates product unveilings, product managers must understand that communication is the foundation upon which their product's success rests. Whether it's presenting a compelling product vision to the team or translating user feedback into actionable improvements, it all hinges on effective communication.

Linking Effective Communication to Product Success

Take Airbnb as an example. The success of their platform isn't just about connecting hosts and guests; it's about how they communicate the unique experiences users can have. Effective communication can transform a simple concept into a global phenomenon.

In the world of product management, the success of a product is intricately linked to how well it's communicated. Without effective communication, even the most innovative features may remain overlooked. Whether it's in marketing the product's benefits to potential users or in conveying its value to internal teams, communication is the bridge that connects product potential to its realization.

The Art of Conveying a Compelling Product Vision

Tesla's journey is a testament to the power of a compelling product vision. Beyond just manufacturing electric cars, they've effectively communicated a vision of sustainability, innovation, and a better future. It's not just about selling vehicles; it's about selling a dream.

Product managers are the torchbearers of a product's vision. Much like Elon Musk conveys a vision of revolutionizing transportation, product managers must master the art of conveying where their product is headed and why it matters. It's about inspiring stakeholders, team members, and users by narrating a story of how the product makes a difference in their lives.

Communicating with Stakeholders

Effective communication with stakeholders is the cornerstone that ensures everyone involved in the product journey is on the same page. It's about understanding who your stakeholders are, what they need, and how to engage with them.

Identifying and Engaging Key Stakeholders in Product Development

Think of Amazon's approach to stakeholder engagement. They don't just cater to customers; they actively engage with third-party sellers, recognizing them as essential participants. This comprehensive approach illustrates the importance of recognizing and engaging all relevant stakeholders in your product's journey.

Identifying key stakeholders is the first step. These can include customers, executives, development teams, marketers, and more. Effective communication means understanding the unique needs and expectations of each stakeholder group, just as Amazon tailors its communication to cater to the specific requirements of sellers, buyers, and partners.

Techniques for Aligning Product Objectives with Stakeholder Interests

Salesforce excels at aligning product objectives with stakeholder interests. Their "Customer 360" vision not only meets customer needs but also addresses the interests of various stakeholders, from sales teams to IT departments. Effective communication bridges the gap between diverse interests.

In the world of product management, success hinges on aligning the product's objectives with the interests of stakeholders. This alignment can be achieved through clear and persuasive communication. We'll explore techniques for conveying how the product not only serves users but also meets the goals and expectations of internal and external stakeholders.

Stakeholder Management and Expectations

Just as Disney manages various stakeholder interests, from park visitors to shareholders, effective product managers must also manage expectations. Disney's success lies in delivering consistent and memorable experiences, and communication plays a crucial role in achieving this.

Product managers act as the bridge between different stakeholder groups, ensuring their expectations are understood and addressed. This involves managing expectations by providing realistic timelines, transparent communication, and effective feedback loops.

In the upcoming sections, we'll delve deeper into collaborative cross-functional communication, strategies for navigating challenging conversations, and the significance of effective documentation practices. These elements collectively form the foundation of effective communication in the dynamic world of product management.

Collaborative Cross-Functional Communication

In the world of product management, no endeavor is accomplished in isolation. It's a collaborative dance, and effective communication ensures that all the players are in sync. This section explores how to facilitate seamless communication and collaboration across diverse teams and departments.

Nurturing Collaboration Between Product Managers, Designers, Engineers, and Other Teams

Consider the success story of Slack. Their communication platform thrives because it doesn't just connect users; it connects product managers, designers, engineers, and countless other teams who work together to deliver a top-notch product. This collaboration is the result of effective cross-functional communication.

Collaboration starts with effective communication between product managers and cross-functional teams. It's about breaking down silos and fostering an environment where ideas, feedback, and information flow freely. Just as Slack brings people together through its platform, product managers bring teams together through effective communication.

Effective Methods for Cross-Functional Communication and Collaboration

Tesla's innovations are a testament to the power of cross-functional collaboration. From engineers to designers to marketing teams, their collective efforts drive product excellence. Effective communication and collaboration are the engines that power their success.

In product management, it's vital to use effective methods for cross-functional communication. This includes regular meetings, agile methodologies like Scrum, and collaboration tools. We'll delve into the techniques that bridge gaps and streamline communication between different departments, ensuring everyone works in harmony to achieve a common goal.

Achieving a Shared Vision and Understanding Across Departments

Just as Google's suite of products reflects a shared vision of organizing information, product managers need to cultivate a shared vision across departments. Effective communication ensures that every team understands the product's purpose and the role they play in its success.

Achieving a shared vision is about aligning departments, whether it's development, marketing, or sales, to a common set of goals.

Exercise

Effective communication and collaboration are the lifeblood of successful product management. As future product managers, you will find yourself in situations where you must facilitate smooth communication across various teams and departments to achieve your project goals. This business case study presents scenarios to analyze and make informed decisions that demonstrate your understanding of the vital concepts of promoting seamless cross-team communication.

Scenario 1: Interdepartmental Alignment

You are tasked with developing a new mobile app for your company. The marketing team has a specific vision for the app's user interface, while the development team has its own technical requirements. How will you ensure that these two departments are aligned, working towards the same goal, and speaking the same language?

Workspace:

Scenario 2: External Vendor Collaboration

Your project requires integrating a complex third-party solution. You need to collaborate with an external vendor to ensure the integration goes smoothly. However, your technical team is skeptical about the vendor's capabilities. How will you bridge the gap between your team's concerns and the vendor's promises to establish a productive partnership?

Workspace:

Scenario 3: Cross-Functional Product Launch

Your product is about to launch, and it involves multiple teams, from development to marketing and sales. How will you coordinate the efforts of these cross-functional teams to ensure a synchronized product launch, including feature highlights, marketing campaigns, and sales enablement?

Workspace:

Scenario 4: Stakeholder Expectations

Stakeholders from different departments have conflicting expectations about the project's timeline and scope. How will you address these conflicting interests and communicate a realistic plan that meets the project's objectives and balances the stakeholders' needs?

Workspace:

Scenario 5: Feedback Incorporation

You've gathered user feedback, which includes valuable insights from your customer support team. However, your development team is resistant to making the suggested changes, fearing delays. How will you navigate this situation to ensure that user feedback is effectively incorporated without causing friction within your team?

Workspace:

Navigating difficult conversations

Difficult conversations are a common part of the product management journey. Whether you are resolving conflicts within your team or discussing major shifts with stakeholders, handling these talks with diplomacy and tact is crucial. In this section, we will explore how to prepare for these challenging discussions to ensure they lead to positive outcomes.

Recognizing and Addressing Challenges and Conflicts in Product Management

Imagine this: You are in the middle of a project, and suddenly, tensions start brewing among team members. You notice that they have disagreements about the product's direction. In response, don't let the issues fester; instead, take proactive steps. You initiate a meeting to address the issues openly.

The result? By addressing the situation and facilitating open communication, you were able to resolve the conflicts and refocus the team on the project's goals.

Strategies for Handling Tough Conversations with Diplomacy and Tact

Now: picture a project meeting where team members have differing opinions about a critical feature. The atmosphere is tense, and it is clear that a diplomatic approach is needed. So, you actively listen to each team member's perspective, giving them the space to share their thoughts.

The outcome? By creating a space for open discussion, the team reaches a consensus, and the project moves forward with a clear direction.

Ensuring Productive Outcomes from Difficult Discussions

Lastly, let's talk about a heated discussion with a stakeholder regarding project timelines. Things were becoming confrontational. What did you do? You took a step back and refocused on your shared goals. You reminded everyone involved of the project Is shared objectives and emphasized the importance of collaboration.

The impact? The tone of the conversation shifted from confrontational to collaborative, leading to a more productive discussion and alignment on project goals.

In the world of product management, the ability to navigate tough conversations is a valuable skill. Whether you're managing a team, dealing with stakeholders, or addressing user concerns, using a human touch and empathetic approach can lead to better product outcomes and successful collaborations.

Exercise

As future product managers, you will often encounter scenarios that demand skillful navigation of challenging conversations to ensure successful project outcomes. In this business case study, we present real-world scenarios that provide opportunities for analysis and decision-making, emphasizing the importance of diplomacy, tact, and effective communication.

Scenario 1: Feature Prioritization

You are the product manager for a software project. Your development team is convinced that implementing a specific feature is crucial for the product is success. However, a senior stakeholder from the finance department vehemently opposes it and insists that resources should be directed toward a different feature. This scenario prompts you to carefully orchestrate a discussion that bridges the gap and leads to a resolution that maximizes the product is potential. How will you approach this delicate negotiation to align your team's diverse perspectives.

Workspace:

Scenario 2: Timeline Realignment

Your team is diligently working toward a challenging deadline for the launch of a new product. Unexpected technical challenges have emerged, casting doubt on the feasibility of meeting the original timeline. You now face the daunting task of communicating this to stakeholders who have set their expectations based on the initial launch date. This scenario necessitates a strategic approach to managing stakeholder reactions while maintaining their trust in your team is competence. How will you navigate this high-stakes conversation?

Workspace:

Scenario 3: Budget Constraints

Midway through your project, you uncover budget constraints that could impact the scope of the project. Your stakeholders have enthusiastically endorsed the original project plan and have high expectations for its features and functionalities. You are tasked with conveying this unexpected development without eroding the trust they have in your project management capabilities. How will you communicate this financial setback and realign stakeholder expectations to preserve project integrity?

Workspace:

Scenario 4: User Feedback Disagreements

User feedback from beta testing suggests that a significant change in product direction may be necessary to effectively meet users needs. However, the leadership team harbors concern regarding potential delays and resource reassignment. This scenario requires you to strike a balance between satisfying user requirements and respecting organizational constraints. How will you navigate this pivotal conversation, aligning user interests with the broader strategic objectives of the organization?

Workspace:

Scenario 5: Vendor Selection

Your team is in the critical phase of vendor selection for a key component of a project. Team members hold diverse and strongly held preferences for different vendors, leading to internal conflicts that jeopardize the objectivity of the selection process. This scenario requires your intervention to mediate internal tensions and ensure a rational and unbiased vendor selection that aligns with the project is best interests. How will you manage this internal discord to ensure a fair and informed choice?

Workspace:

Effective Documentation Practices

In the world of product management, documentation becomes your dependable companion, helping you make sense of the dynamic landscape. Let's explore why documentation is crucial and how it serves as a vital tool in product management. Additionally, we will discuss the significance of shared work notes and organized folders dedicated to project-specific insights and customer interviews for the entire product management team.

The Importance of Clear and Comprehensive Documentation in Product Management

Think of documentation as the storyteller of your product's narrative. The narrator captures your product's evolution, from inception to realization. Like a journal, it keeps you grounded and provides context for future endeavors.

For example, a well-known software company

This company deeply understands the value of documentation. They maintain extensive records of customer interactions, order histories, and product details. This comprehensive documentation not only aids in providing excellent customer service but also drives data-driven decision-making. Meticulous documentation is a key factor in their ability to continuously improve their services.

Documenting Requirements, specifications, and Project Progress

In the complex world of product management, documentation takes various forms. It starts with documenting user requirements, the foundation upon which your product is built. These requirements are then transformed into detailed specifications, providing a clear roadmap for your development team. Additionally, documentation serves as a journal of your project's progress, recording the twists and turns along the way.

For instance, a leading cloud computing service provider

This provider stands as a stellar example of effective documentation. They offer a vast library of documentation, including detailed user guides, API references, and case studies. This extensive documentation empowers developers to effectively understand and leverage their services. It's a testament to how meticulous documentation can enhance user experience and foster a thriving developer community.

Best Practices for Maintaining Organized and Accessible Documentation

In the dynamic world of product management, organized and accessible documentation is the foundation of success. It ensures that your documentation remains a living resource, rather than a stagnant archive. Best practices involve structuring and categorizing your documentation for easy access and navigation.

For instance, shared work notes with dedicated project folders and customer interview repositories

An innovative technology company provides an excellent example of this practice. Their employees have access to shared work notes that include project-specific folders and a customer interviews repository. This organized approach enhances productivity and knowledge sharing across the entire product management team.

In the world of product management, documentation is more than just a record-keeper; it's a collaborator, an enabler of decisions, and a unifying force. By understanding the importance of clear and comprehensive documentation and incorporating shared work notes with dedicated folders for project-specific insights and customer interview, product managers can navigate their path with precision and clarity.

Case: Enhancing Documentation Practices at a Leading Cloud Provider

This business case outlines the need to enhance documentation practices at a leading cloud provider, led by Abhi. Effective documentation is paramount for delivering quality services, improving user experiences, and fostering a thriving developer community. By investing in comprehensive and organized documentation, our organization can further solidify its position as a cloud computing leader and drive continuous improvement.

Background

Abhi, a seasoned product manager at a leading cloud provider, recognized the pivotal role of documentation in their organization's success. Over the years, the company has thrived by offering innovative cloud services to a diverse client base, including developers, businesses, and enterprises. Documentation has been a fundamental tool in this journey, enabling clients to effectively utilize our services and empowering our internal teams to make data-driven decisions.

However, with the company's rapid growth, Abhi observed that the existing documentation practices were facing challenges. The sheer volume of information, including user guides, API references, and case studies, was overwhelming. Disorganized documentation hampered the team's efficiency, slowed down onboarding of new employees, and occasionally led to inconsistencies in customer support.

Objective

The primary objective of this initiative is to enhance documentation practices within the organization, thereby:

1. Ensuring that documentation remains comprehensive and up to date, meeting the evolving needs of our clients and internal teams.

2. Organizing the documentation into structured, accessible folders to facilitate swift information retrieval.

3. Improving knowledge sharing across the product management team through shared work notes and repositories dedicated to project-specific insights and customer interviews.

Proposed Solution

To address these challenges, Abhi proposes the following solutions:

1. Documentation Overhaul: Abhi suggests conducting a comprehensive review of the existing documentation, updating, and augmenting it as necessary to ensure its relevance and completeness.

2. Structured Folders: The introduction of structured folders within the documentation repository will allow for easy access to specific information, such as project-specific insights and customer interviews.

3. Shared Work notes: Abhi envisions the implementation of shared work notes for the product management team, fostering seamless knowledge sharing and collaboration.

Benefits

The proposed solutions offer several key benefits:

1. Enhanced User Experience: Updated and comprehensive documentation will empower users to better understand and utilize our services, resulting in improved user experiences.

2. Improved Productivity: Structured folders and shared work notes will increase team productivity and efficiency by providing quick access to relevant information.

3. Knowledge Sharing: The shared work notes will promote knowledge sharing and collaboration among the product management team, enhancing problem-solving capabilities and decision-making.

4. Competitive Advantage: An organized, accessible, and up-to-date documentation system will solidify our position as a cloud computing leader, attracting more users, and fostering loyalty.

Financial Impact

While the financial impact is harder to quantify directly, the proposed improvements are expected to result in a return on investment in the form of increased user retention, reduced support costs, and enhanced user acquisition.

Conclusion

Enhancing documentation practices at our leading cloud provider, under Abhi's leadership, is crucial for sustaining our position in the industry. By investing in a comprehensive and organized documentation system, the organization can ensure that its users have an exceptional experience while enabling the product management team to work more effectively and collaboratively. This initiative aligns perfectly with our mission of providing exceptional cloud services and continuous improvement.

Describe the image with clear labels and roles.

7 BUILDING TEAMS

Welcome to the chapter that explores the core of successful product management—constructing and nurturing high-achieving teams. In the domain of product management, the product manager is the guide, and the team is the driving force. The product manager defines the vision, but it's the team's collaborative efforts and creative input bring that vision to life. This chapter is a venture into understanding the dynamics, methods, and skills needed to craft a team that not only grasps your vision but also contributes their unique perspectives to product development. From the nuances of recruitment and orientation to empowering and inspiring your team, and even handling the intricacies of remote collaboration, we will uncover the multi-faceted universe of building and leading high-performing product teams. Let us commence this exploration and may your product teams thrive like a well-synchronized team.

The Importance of Team Dynamics

In product management, the driving force behind successful endeavors is not just the individual brilliance of the product manager but the collective synergy of the product team.

Imagine a well-coordinated sports team where each player knows their position, strengths, and how to collaborate seamlessly with their teammates. In product management, a high-performing team is akin to a sports team—every member has a crucial role, understands their responsibilities, and functions cohesively to achieve common goals.

Enhanced Productivity and Innovation

Cohesive team dynamics lead to enhanced productivity and innovation. When team members work smoothly together, ideas flow more freely, creativity is nurtured, and problem-solving becomes a collaborative effort. Productivity soars as members support and complement one another's skills.

> For example, a software development team at a tech startup consistently meets or exceeds project deadlines because they have established a work environment where open communication, trust, and collaboration are the norms. This has led to innovative solutions and efficient product development.

Emotional Intelligence and Team Cohesion

Emotional intelligence is a binding force of team cohesion. It involves recognizing, understanding, and effectively managing emotions, both one's own and those of others. Product managers play a vital role in fostering emotional intelligence within the team by leading with empathy and understanding.

> Consider a product manager who listens actively to team members, acknowledges their concerns, and celebrates their achievements. This not only boosts team morale but also strengthens the emotional bonds that contribute to cohesive team dynamics.

Fostering Trust and Open Communication

Trust is the foundation of any productive team. In an environment where team members trust one another, they feel safe to express their opinions, share their insights, and admit when they need assistance. Open communication, in turn, becomes the lifeblood of a collaborative team.

A product team working on a complex project actively encourages open communication and values honest feedback. Team members are not afraid to voice their ideas or concerns, leading to faster issue resolution and improved project outcomes.

Strategies for Fostering Trust and Open Communication within the Team

As a product manager, it's your responsibility to create an environment where trust and open communication thrive. Here are some strategies to foster these essential qualities within your team:

1. Lead by example:

To cultivate trust and open communication, start by leading by example. Demonstrate transparency, honesty, and a willingness to listen. When team members observe these qualities in their product manager, they are more likely to mirror them.

2. Establish clear expectations:

Set clear expectations for your team regarding communication, feedback, and collaboration. Define roles, responsibilities, and reporting structures, so that everyone knows how they fit into the larger picture. Clarity reduces uncertainty and enhances trust.

3. Encourage active listening:

Active listening is crucial for effective communication. Encourage team members to listen attentively to one another, ask clarifying questions, and demonstrate that their input is valued. This not only promotes trust but also ensures that information is thoroughly understood.

4. Create a safe space:

Team members should feel safe expressing their thoughts, ideas, and concerns without fear of judgment. Encourage a culture where no question is too small, and no idea is too insignificant to be discussed. When individuals know that their voices are heard and respected, trust naturally develops.

5.   Feedback as a two-way street:

Feedback is a powerful tool for growth and improvement. Emphasize that feedback should flow in both directions—top-down and bottom-up. Product managers should provide constructive feedback, but they should also actively seek input and feedback from team members.

6.   Celebrate achievements:

Acknowledging and celebrating team achievements, whether big or small, fosters a sense of recognition and accomplishment. This positive reinforcement contributes to a more supportive and trusting environment.

7.   Constructively resolve conflicts:

Conflicts are a natural part of team dynamics. However, they should be resolved constructively. Encourage team members to address conflicts openly and collaboratively, focusing on finding solutions rather than assigning blame.

8.   Regular team building:

Periodic team-building activities and exercises can help strengthen bonds and build trust. These activities can be both fun and educational, encouraging team members to get to know each other better outside of the regular work environment.

9.   Use collaboration tools:

Leverage collaboration tools and technologies to facilitate communication within the team, particularly if you have remote or distributed team members. Tools such as messaging apps, project management software, and video conferencing platforms can enhance connectivity.

10. Feedback channels:

Create formalized feedback channels where team members can submit anonymous feedback or suggestions if they are uncomfortable sharing openly. This allows for honest input without fear of repercussions.

By implementing these strategies, you can cultivate a culture of trust and open communication within your product team. The result is a harmonious and motivated team that collaborates effectively and drives the success of your product development efforts.

Team Roles and Collaboration in Product Management

Creating a Unified Product Team

In the exciting field of product management, the real magic happens when a group of diverse individuals come together, each with their unique role, to create something exceptional. Think of it as a thrilling performance where everyone has a part to play, and the product manager, well, they're the leader, ensuring everything flows smoothly.

Understanding Different Team Roles

Product teams are like a skilled sports team, with each member playing a different position. Here's a quick look at the key players:

- Product Manager: The visionary leader who sets the stage and ensures everyone's on the same page.

- UX/UI Designers: The creative minds who craft the product's look and feel.

- Developers: The technical experts who transform ideas into reality.

- QA Testers: The quality control experts who ensure the final product is flawless.

- Marketers: The storytellers who bring the product to the world's attention.

- Sales and Customer Support: The frontline experts who understand customers and their needs.

- Data Analysts: The number crunchers who provide insights from user data.

Effective Collaboration Techniques

Now, imagine these diverse talents working seamlessly together, like a skilled sports team, each playing their part with expertise. Here's how to make it happen:

- Cross-Functional Teams: Mix and match players from different departments to get fresh perspectives and solutions.

- Foster Communication: Encourage everyone to talk openly, share ideas, and provide feedback. Regular meetings and collaboration tools help this process.

- Collaborative Decision-Making: Sometimes, the best decisions come from brainstorming sessions and open discussions. Don't be afraid to seek input from all players.

- Design Thinking Workshops: Organize workshops where team members can get creative and share their wildest product ideas.

- Regular Feedback Loops: Create spaces for everyone to voice their opinions, such as sprint reviews or feedback sessions.

- Prototyping and Ideation: Visualize your ideas together through prototypes and brainstorming sessions.

- Conflict Resolution: When conflicts arise, focus on finding solutions, not assigning blame. It's all part of the creative process.

The Product Manager's Role as Leader

Just like a team captain guides their teammates, the product manager takes the lead. They set the vision, ensure that everyone knows their part, and keep the team on track. They're the bridge between innovation and practicality, ensuring that the team's efforts align with the big picture.

In the end, product management is all about teamwork. Understanding each team member's role, encouraging collaboration, and embracing the product manager's role as the leader will make your product team hum with creativity and efficiency, creating a successful product.

Leveraging Diverse Skills and Perspectives within the Team: Unleashing Creativity

In the multifaceted realm of product management, the kaleidoscope of talents within your team is your greatest asset. Think of it as having a versatile toolkit at your disposal, each tool with its unique function. When effectively harnessed, this diversity of skills and perspectives can be the driving force behind your product's success. Let's dive into the art of maximizing the potential of these diverse elements.

Celebrate Individual Strengths:

Within your product team, there's a combination of skills and talents. UX/UI designers bring esthetics and user-centric design to the forefront, developers provide the technical backbone, marketers understand the psychology of your audience, and data analysts unlock insights from numbers. Celebrate these individual strengths, recognizing the unique value each team member brings to the table. This acknowledgment fosters a sense of belonging and appreciation, driving motivation and creativity.

Meet Sarah, the UX/UI designer in a product team. Her unique skill set allows her to visualize and create user-friendly interfaces. The product manager, Mark, recognizes Sarah's talent and empowers her to lead the design process. With her skills celebrated, Sarah feels a deep sense of ownership in the team, resulting in innovative and visually appealing product designs that resonate with users.

Balance Creativity and Practicality:

Every team member has a unique risk appetite. Some thrive on creative innovation, while others anchor the team in practicality and reliability. Embrace these differences, and create a harmonious equilibrium between visionary thinking and feasible implementation. After all, a brilliant idea becomes a game-changer only when it can be executed effectively. The interplay between these diverse approaches can spark remarkable product solutions.

In Tom's product development team, there's a friendly clash of perspectives. Tom, a developer, and Emma, a marketer, represent the creative and practical sides of the project, respectively. Rather than letting this clash create tension, they've learned to collaborate. Tom's innovative ideas are balanced with Emma's practical approach. The result? A product that's both visionary and executable, finding a sweet spot between creativity and practicality.

Embrace Diverse Perspectives:

Diversity isn't just about skills; it's also about the array of perspectives and backgrounds your team members bring. Welcome and encourage open dialogs where every voice, regardless of its origin, can be heard and valued. It's often in the fusion of various ideas and viewpoints that truly innovative solutions emerge. This mosaic of perspectives becomes a source of your team's collective intelligence.

Within David's product team, there's a rich diversity of backgrounds and experiences. Sarah brings user empathy from her psychology background, John offers a technical viewpoint, and Rina, with her international experience, provides global market insights. By encouraging open dialog and valuing these different perspectives, the team identifies unique solutions that resonate with a broad and diverse user base.

Collaborative Problem-Solving:

The richness of diverse skills and perspectives isn't fully realized until your team collaborates effectively. Encourage members to join forces when tackling challenges. Different angles and approaches are essential for tackling complex problems from multiple perspective. Collaborative problem-solving not only enhances the quality of solutions but also fosters a sense of collective ownership.

When a complex technical issue arises in Mary's product team, the team comes together rather than assigning blame. Developers, QA testers, and data analysts collaboratively analyze the problem from their unique angles. This approach leads to a swift resolution and strengthens the sense of shared responsibility within the team.

Continuous Learning and Development:

To maintain this diverse tapestry of skills and perspectives, champion a culture of continuous learning and personal growth within your team. Encourage team members to stay updated on industry trends, invest in their professional development, and share their newfound knowledge with the team. This ongoing development not only benefits individuals but also elevates the collective knowledge and capabilities of your product team.

In Alex's product team, continuous learning is a shared value. Team members are encouraged to attend workshops, webinars, and conferences to stay updated on industry trends. Recently, their data analyst, Jake, attended a data analytic seminar and provided insights that transformed their approach. The culture of learning not only benefits individual team members but keeps the whole team at the forefront of industry advancements.

By wholeheartedly embracing the diverse skills and perspectives within your team, you are essentially tapping into a wellspring of innovation and adaptability. Every team member is a vital contributor, and when their strengths are combined, they become a powerful driving force propelling your product toward excellence. Remember, it's the fusion of these unique elements that creates a product's true brilliance.

Hiring and Onboarding

In product management, there's no substitute for having the right team by your side. It's like assembling a group of trusted companions for a shared mission. The success of your endeavor hinges on the quality of your team and how seamlessly they integrate into the task at hand. This section is all about the art of attracting the finest talent, conducting interviews and assessments that work, and ensuring a smooth boarding process for the newest members of your team.

Recruiting and boarding are the foundational steps that lay the groundwork for your product team's performance. Finding the perfect individuals and ensure they transition smoothly into your team isn't just about ticking boxes; it's about orchestrating a harmonious ensemble. So, let's embark on this cooperative exploration together, discovering how to build your dream product team and set the stage for success in the dynamic world of product management.

Recruitment Strategies for Assembling a Top-Tier Product Team

The success of your team begins with finding the right individuals who not only have the necessary skills but also share your vision and values. To do this, you need a well-thought-out recruitment strategy. Here, we'll delve into key strategies for assembling a top-tier product team:

Define Clear Job Descriptions:

Clarity is your ally. Start by creating job descriptions that are detailed and transparent. Clearly outline the roles, responsibilities, and expectations of each team member. By doing this, you'll attract candidates who resonate with your mission and who know what they're signing up for.

Leverage Multiple Recruitment Channels:

Don't limit your search to one place. Spread your net wide by using a combination of job boards, social networks, personal referrals, and even attending industry events. Each channel can bring different talents and experiences to your doorstep.

To attract a diverse pool of candidates, post your job openings on multiple platforms. Use *LinkedIn* for professional networking, *Indeed* for a wide job-seeker audience, and industry-specific job boards such as *Behance* for design roles. Tools such as Jobvite or Greenhouse can help you manage job postings across multiple platforms from a single dashboard.

Assess Cultural Fit:

Skills are important, but culture matters just as much. Your team should share values, goals, and working styles. When assessing candidates, evaluate not only their technical prowess but also how well they align with your team's culture.

Imagine you're hiring for a startup with a fast-paced, innovative culture. During interviews, ask questions like, "Tell us about a time when you had to adapt quickly to a changing situation." To assess cultural fit, use tools such as culture assessment surveys, such as the one provided by Culture Amp, which gathers feedback from your team to understand the existing culture and what candidates might add to it.

Behavioral Interviews:

Behavioral interviews are a powerful tool for understanding how candidates have handled situations in the past. By asking them to share specific examples of their experiences, you can gain insights into how they might perform in your team. Look for adaptability, problem-solving, and collaborative skills.

When interviewing a candidate for a project manager role, present a scenario like, "Describe a time when a project faced unexpected delays. How did you handle it?" Use a structured scorecard or rubric to evaluate their responses consistently. Tools like Workable offer templates for behavioral interview questions and scorecards to streamline the process.

Refine Your Employer Brand:

Just as you're looking for the right candidates, they are also evaluating your organization. Craft a compelling employer brand that highlights your team's culture, mission, and opportunities for growth. A strong employer brand will attract like-minded individuals who are excited to be part of your journey.

Suppose you want to highlight your tech company's commitment to innovation. Showcase case studies of successful projects on your website and social media. Leverage employee advocacy tools such as Bambu to encourage team members to share their positive experiences. Use branding tools like Canva to create visually appealing content that aligns with your employer brand.

With these recruitment strategies in your toolkit, you're better equipped to attract top talent. Remember, your team is only as strong as its members, so put your best foot forward when building your product management dream team.

Conducting Effective Interviews and Assessments

In talent acquisition, conducting interviews and assessments is where you dive deeper into understanding a candidate's potential. It's the phase where you determine whether the person sitting across from you is not just a good fit but an exceptional one for your product team. Let's explore four essential strategies to ensure your interviews and assessments lead to making the right choices.

Implementing Structured Interviews:

Structured interviews are your dependable compass when it comes to evaluating potential candidates for your product team. They provide a systematic and fair approach for assessing each candidate. Here, we'll dive into the practical aspect of implementing structured interviews with real-world examples and the tools that can streamline the process.

Let's say you're hiring a User experience (UX) Designer for your software development team. In a structured interview, you will create a set of specific, job-related questions designed to evaluate the candidate's skills, experience, and alignment with your team's culture. For instance, you might ask:

"Can you describe a project where you had to balance user preferences with technical constraints? How did you manage this challenge?"

"Tell us about a time when you redesigned an existing product to improve its user experience. What were the key steps you took?"

Tools to Facilitate Structured Interviews:

1. Google Forms: You can create customized interview templates

in Google Forms, with questions and scoring criteria. This tool ensures that each interviewer asks the same set of questions, promoting consistency.

2. Greenhouse: Greenhouse is a comprehensive applicant tracking system that includes structured interview features. It allows you to design interview kits, score candidates, and gather feedback from multiple interviewers efficiently.

3. Trello: Trello is a visual collaboration tool that can help you organize and manage your structured interviews. You can create boards for each candidate, outline the interview questions, and track progress.

4. Asana: Asana provides project management tools that can be adapted for structured interviews. Create a project for each candidate, list the interview questions as tasks, and use the comment feature for evaluation and collaboration among interviewers.

Structured interviews ensure that every candidate is assessed using the same set of criteria, thereby reducing bias, and promoting fairness. They also allow you to gather consistent data for objective decision-making. By utilizing practical examples and the right tools, you can make structured interviews a valuable compass guiding you to the best additions to your product team.

Using Behavioral Questions:

Behavioral questions are like a window into a candidate's past experiences and actions. By asking these specific questions, you gain valuable insights into problem-solving skills, adaptability, and their potential fit within your product team. Let's delve into the practical aspect of using behavioral questions with real-world examples and tools that can assist in the process.

Suppose you're interviewing a candidate for a Project Manager role on your product team. You want to understand how they handle challenges and conflicts. You could ask:

"Tell us about a time when a project you were leading faced

unexpected delays. How did you identify the issue, and what steps did you take to get the project back on track?"

"Share an example of a situation in which you had to coordinate a cross-functional team with conflicting priorities. How did you manage to align everyone toward a common goal?"

Tools to Facilitate Behavioral Questions:

1. InterviewBuddy: InterviewBuddy is an online platform that provides a library of behavioral interview questions. It can help you create customized interview scripts based on the role you're hiring for.

2. HireVue: HireVue offers an AI-driven interview platform that includes behavioral questions. It allows candidates to record video responses, which you can review at your convenience.

3. Lever: Lever is an applicant tracking system that offers a structured interview feature. It allows you to design interview kits with behavioral questions and share them with your team for consistent evaluations.

4. Prevue: Prevue provides a suite of assessment tools, including behavioral questions. It offers candidate reports that help you understand how a candidate's behaviors align with the demands of your role.

Behavioral questions offer a glimpse into a candidate's past actions and decision-making, allowing you to assess how they might handle similar situations in the future.

Employing Skills Assessments:

When it comes to hiring for your product team, skills assessments are like a hands-on test drive. They provide tangible evidence of a candidate's abilities and ensure that they possess the practical skills needed for the role. Let's explore the practical side of employing skills assessments with real-world examples and tools that can make the process more effective.

Suppose you're hiring a software developer. To assess their coding skills, you may provide a coding challenge. For instance, you could ask the candidate to write a program that sorts a list of numbers in Python. This practical task not only evaluates their coding proficiency but also their problem-solving skills.

Tools for Facilitating Skills Assessments:

1. Codewars: Codewars is an online platform that offers coding challenges and kata. You can create custom coding challenges or use existing ones to assess a candidate's coding skills.

2. TestDome: TestDome provides a wide range of skill assessment tests for technical roles. It includes coding challenges, multiple-choice questions, and practical exercises.

3. Behance: Behance, a platform for creative professionals, can be used for skills assessments in roles like graphic design or UX/UI design. Candidates can showcase their portfolios, providing evidence of their abilities.

4. GitHub: GitHub can be used for assess a candidate's version control and collaborative coding skills. Reviewing a candidate's GitHub profile can give you insights into their coding style and project contributions.

Skills assessments ensure that a candidate can not only talk the talk but also walk the walk. By using the above, you can effectively incorporate skills assessments into your hiring process, helping you identify team members who have the practical abilities needed for your product team.

Considering Panel Interviews:

Panel interviews involve multiple team members interviewing a candidate simultaneously. They offer diverse perspectives and help in making a comprehensive evaluation. Each panel member can focus on different aspects, such as technical skills, cultural fit, or behavioral attributes.

Imagine you're interviewing a candidate for a Product Manager position. In a panel interview, you could have members from different areas, such as engineering, design, and marketing, participate. Each panel member can focus on specific aspects. For instance:

- The engineering team member can assess the candidate's technical understanding.
- The design team member can evaluate their user-centric approach.
- The marketing team member can gauge their product strategy and market alignment.

This multifaceted approach ensures a holistic evaluation.

Tools for Facilitating Panel Interviews:

1. Zoom: Zoom is a widely used video conferencing tool that can help you set up virtual panel interviews. It allows you to invite multiple panel members and candidates for a seamless discussion.

2. Microsoft Teams: Microsoft Teams offers similar features for virtual panel interviews. You can schedule and conduct interviews while collaborating with your team in real-time.

3. Slack: Slack can be used to coordinate panel interview. You can create channels for different interview rounds, share candidate information, and allow panel members to discuss and provide feedback.

4. Google Meet: Google Meet provides video conferencing capabilities that work well for panel interviews. It integrates with Google Calendar for scheduling and organization.

Panel interviews give you a 360-degree view of a candidate, offering various insights into their potential fit for your product team. By using practical examples and the right tools, you can effectively implement panel interviews, ensuring that your hiring decisions are comprehensive and well-informed.

Streamlining the Onboarding Process for New Team Members

Introducing new team members to your product management journey is a pivotal moment. It's akin to welcoming a new member to your group - their role is essential to the overall performance. An effective boarding process is the blueprint that ensures they seamlessly integrate into your team and contribute effectively.

In this section, we'll delve into the art of simplifying the boarding process. It's not just about making it easy; it's about making it a valuable experience. We'll discuss how to provide clear, helpful documentation, establish mentorship programs, offer practical training, schedule regular feedback sessions, and create an inclusive and welcoming atmosphere. With each of these components, you'll create a harmonious boarding process that enhances your product management journey.

Providing Clear Documentation

In effective product management, the adventure begins when new team members join the ranks. Just as well-constructed guide leads travelers through unfamiliar terrain, clear documentation is the cornerstone of successful onboarding. It's the key to helping newcomers navigate the landscape of your organization. This section explores the art of creating comprehensive and user-friendly resources and offers real-world examples of well-structured boarding documents.

Creating Comprehensive and User-Friendly Resources:

Initiating a thorough boarding experience starts with well-crafted documentation. These resources serve as guides for new team members. They should offer an in-depth view of your organization's mission, values, and the specifics of their roles and responsibilities.

User-friendly resources are those that are easy to access and understand. Whether it's through digital handbooks, instructive video tutorials, or a combination of both, accessibility ensures that these valuable resources are readily available.

Examples of Well-Structured Onboarding Documents:

- Employee Handbooks: Think of these as the anchor document, the comprehensive guide to company policies, procedures, and culture, ensuring everyone is on the same page.

- Process Guides: In roles that involve specific workflows, these guides provide step-by-step instructions and best practices, simplifying complex tasks.

- Training Videos: Visual learning can be highly effective. Videos that elucidate company culture or software usage can be like having a friendly mentor by your side.

- Checklists: A straightforward yet impactful tool, checklists allow new team members to track their progress through the onboarding process.

- FAQ Documents: These preemptively answer common questions, reducing confusion and expediting the adaptation journey.

Clear documentation is your treasure trove, guiding new team members through the intricate landscape of your organization. By providing accessible and detailed resources, you empower your new hires to not only find their way but to thrive within your product management team.

Establishing Mentorship Programs

Crafting mentorship programs is much like preparing a well-marked path for newcomers. These programs should be purposeful and organized, offering a series of activities and interactions that foster learning, connection, and personal growth. It could involve things like new hires shadowing experienced colleagues, participating in training sessions, or simply having regular one-on-one conversations with their mentors.

The Role of Mentors in Onboarding:

Mentors are like the experienced travelers who accompany

newcomers on their journey. They provide insights, guidance, and a friendly presence to ensure that new hires feel comfortable and supported. Mentors play a crucial role by:

- Sharing Wisdom: They impart knowledge and insights, helping new hires understand the organization's culture, processes, and expectations.

- Skill Development: Mentors recognize where new hires need skill improvement and offer guidance on how to acquire those skills.

- Cultural Integration: They aid new team members in becoming part of the company culture and help them build meaningful connections.

- Emotional Support: Mentors are a listening ear and a source of emotional support, making the onboarding journey smoother and less overwhelming.

The Need for Incentives:

Incentivizing mentors is about recognizing and appreciating their invaluable contribution. While mentorship often provides intangible rewards, such as personal fulfillment and skill development, concrete incentives can further motivate and acknowledge mentors' efforts. These incentives might include:

1. Recognition: Publicly acknowledging mentors' contributions within the organization, through awards or special events.

2. Professional Development: Offering opportunities for mentors to expand their skills and knowledge, which can benefit their own career growth.

3. Monetary Rewards: Providing financial incentives, bonuses, or other forms of compensation as a token of appreciation.

Designing Incentive Programs:

Creating a structured incentive program around mentorship is like setting up a rewards system for your mentors. This can include:

- Clear Criteria: Defining what it takes to be a successful mentor and how one qualifies for incentives.

- Feedback Mechanisms: Implementing regular feedback loops that allow mentees to share their experiences and mentors to assess their own performance.

- Customized Incentives: Tailoring incentives to suit the preferences and needs of mentors, recognizing that not all individuals are motivated by the same rewards.

Incentivizing mentors is about nurturing a mentorship culture that is both fulfilling and rewarding. It's a win-win situation where mentors receive recognition and benefits, while mentees gain guidance and support. As a product manager, understanding the need to incentivize mentors and crafting effective incentive programs is key to ensuring the sustainability and success of your mentorship endeavors.

Hands-on Training:

Hands-on training begins from day one. It involves allowing new team members to work on real tasks, albeit with guidance. For example, if you're introducing a project management tool, assign them a small project and let them explore the tool's features. This kind of experience is invaluable and provides a chance to apply what they've learned immediately.

Another effective method is to create simulated scenarios where new hires can practice handling real-life situations. For instance, a simulated customer support scenario can help them understand how to respond to common customer inquiries.

Pairing new hires with experienced team members is an excellent way to impart practical knowledge. They can observe, ask questions, and gradually take on more responsibility.

Incorporating Interactive Learning Experiences:

1. Role-Playing: Role-playing exercises can simulate various

workplace situations. This can be particularly useful in developing communication skills, like handling challenging client interactions.

2. Case Studies: Real-world case studies allow new team members to apply their knowledge to solve actual problems. This is a powerful way to deepen their understanding of complex topics.

3. Gamification: Turning training into a game can boost engagement. For instance, you can use a gamified app to teach new hires about company policies or product features.

4. Interactive Workshops: Workshops that encourage participation, brainstorming, and group discussions provide a dynamic learning environment. They also foster team collaboration, an essential aspect of product management.

Scheduling Regular Feedback Sessions:

In the ever-evolving landscape of product management, continuous feedback serves as a compass, ensuring that new team members remain on the right track. Ongoing feedback allows them to make real-time adjustments, aligning their roles with the dynamic needs of the team. It boosts confidence by providing recognition for achievements and guidance for areas that require improvement. For instance, using the SBI (Situation, Behavior, Impact) framework, mentors can offer specific examples of situations, describe the observed behavior, and explain the impact on the team or project. These sessions also facilitate cultural assimilation, helping newcomers integrate into the organization's culture and values. In addition, they play a significant role in nurturing relationships. Open and constructive dialogues create trust and respect, both of which are essential for a harmonious team dynamic.

The Framework for Structured Feedback:

Structured feedback sessions are the checkpoints along the journey. They have clear goals, and each session serves a specific purpose, be it tracking progress, addressing challenges, or setting goals for the future. Regularity is essential; scheduled at predetermined intervals, it ensures consistency and stability in the onboarding process. These are not one-sided lectures but rather two-way dialogues. They create a platform for new team members to voice their thoughts, ask questions, and offer suggestions, making feedback a collaborative effort. Keeping records of feedback discussions is a valuable practice. It serves as a reference point for reviewing progress and charting out future growth.

Feedback should be a blend of constructive and positive. It celebrates achievements while offering guidance for improvement, always delivered respectfully and empathetically. These sessions should have clear goals, help new team members set attainable objectives and outline the steps to achieve them. The insights provided should be actionable, offering practical recommendations for growth and development.

Scheduling regular feedback sessions is like having milestones along the journey. They ensure that new team members always know they're on the right path, capable of adapting to changes, and continually evolving in their roles. These sessions empower new hires not only to become confident and effective contributors but also to be integral parts of the product management team's shared success.

Creating a Welcoming and Inclusive Environment

This section delves into the art of creating a welcoming and inclusive environment, emphasizing the significance of building a culture of inclusivity and implementing diversity and inclusion training.

Inclusivity isn't just a buzzword; it's the cornerstone of a productive and harmonious team. It's about ensuring that every member, regardless of their background or perspective, feels respected and valued. Here's how you can build a culture of inclusivity:

Clear Policies: Start by establishing clear policies that promote diversity and inclusion. These policies should be well-defined and communicated effectively to all team members.

Open Communication: Encourage open and honest communication within the team. New members should feel comfortable expressing their ideas, concerns, or questions without fear of discrimination or bias.

Inclusive Events: Organize events and initiatives that celebrate diversity and different perspectives. Whether it's cultural celebrations, guest speakers, or diversity panels, these activities create a sense of belonging and appreciation for the team's diversity.

Equal Opportunities: Ensure that all team members have equal opportunities for growth and advancement. Promotions and recognition should be based on merit and performance, rather than influenced by personal biases or preferences.

Training and Education: Conduct diversity and inclusion training to increase awareness and provide tools for addressing unconscious bias and fostering a diverse and inclusive workplace.

Implementing Diversity and Inclusion Training:

Diversity and inclusion training serves as the compass that helps navigate the complex landscape of differences and perspectives within the team. Implementing effective training involves the following:

Awareness: Begin by creating awareness about the importance of diversity and inclusion. Explain how embracing diversity benefits not only individual team members but also the organization.

Unconscious Bias: Address unconscious bias by educating team members on how to recognize and challenge their own biases and prejudices. This awareness is a critical step toward fostering inclusivity.

Cultural Competency: Provide education on different cultures, backgrounds, and perspectives. Understanding and appreciating diversity within the team fosters a more inclusive and harmonious work environment.

Behavioral Change: Encourage behavioral change through training. The goal is to translate awareness and education into concrete actions that actively promote inclusivity in the workplace.

Regular Updates: Diversity and inclusion training should be an ongoing effort, rather than a one-time event. Regular updates and refresher courses keep everyone engaged and informed about the importance of embracing diversity.

Creating a welcoming and inclusive environment goes beyond mere policy adherence; it requires the adoption of a mindset that values and celebrates differences. When every team member feels welcome and appreciated, they bring their unique perspectives to the table, enriching the product management team and fostering a culture of innovation, collaboration, and respect for all.

Recruitment isn't just about filling positions; it's about finding individuals who not only possess the necessary skills but also align with the team's culture and vision. Effective recruitment ensures that each new member brings a unique perspective, contributing to the diversity and creativity of the team.

Onboarding, on the other hand, sets the tone for a new team member's journey. It's a holistic experience that goes beyond introducing policies and procedures. It's about fostering an environment where every member feels valued, understood, and part of a thriving community. Effective onboarding ensures that team members are equipped with the tools, knowledge, and confidence to excel in their roles.

Empowering and Motivating Your Team

The success of your products isn't solely defined by strategic decisions; it's equally influenced by the spirit and enthusiasm of your team. This section unveils the delicate art of empowering your team members to embrace ownership and initiative, while also implementing powerful motivation techniques to keep their productivity at its peak.

Strategies for Empowering Team Members to Take Ownership and Initiative:

Imagine you're the leader of a diverse and skilled team, ready to navigate uncharted waters. To empower your team, you start by charting a clear course with well-defined objectives. Your vision becomes their guiding star, and each task is imbued with a sense of purpose.

You trust your team with autonomy, granting them the freedom to make decisions in their designated domains. The more they take charge, the stronger the bond of ownership and responsibility. As they hone their skills, their confidence soars, and they are ever more eager to take initiative.

Recognizing their achievements becomes a vital part of your leadership. Just as you acknowledge the strength of the wind or the stars' guidance, you celebrate the milestones they achieve.

Constructive feedback is your compass, steering them in the right direction, are fostering continuous improvement.

Motivation Techniques for Sustaining High Levels of Productivity:

Imagine a skilled leader inspiring their team to perform at its best. Intrinsic motivation is the catalyst that drives each team member. As a leader, you find what resonates with your team members on a personal level. When their hearts align with the goal, their motivation soars.

Together, you set challenging yet achievable goals, akin to creating a masterpiece. These goals become the path that guides their harmonious performance. Feedback is your applause, offered generously to encourage them to improve, and recognition is the standing ovation that fuels their spirits.

Opportunities for growth are the hidden gems that await your team members. Like individuals striving for their spotlight moment, they reach new heights within the team. As the team bonds, they become not just individual players, but a united group.

Balancing Autonomy with Accountability in a Product Team:

As the leader of your initiative, it's crucial to navigate the fine line between autonomy and accountability. With clear expectations set as your compass, you ensure that each team member knows their role and responsibilities. They understand their part in the journey.

Accountability measures become the anchors that keep the initiative steady. As your team exercises autonomy, they're equally aware of the responsibility that accompanies. Your regular check-ins are like guiding lights, offering guidance and support when needed.

You encourage them to solve problems as a collective team, knowing that their shared efforts strengthen the bond and the sense of accountability. Mistakes are embraced as valuable lessons, shaping the journey's narrative, and propelling your team toward greatness.

Managing Remote and Distributed Teams

The COVID-19 pandemic brought about a seismic shift in the way we work, firmly establishing remote and distributed teams as an integral aspect of modern product management. This section delves into the art of managing remote and distributed teams, highlighting unique challenges, the use of tools and technologies for efficient collaboration, and the importance of building trust to maintain cohesion in virtual teams. It also explores the transformative potential of remote work in a post-COVID-19 world.

Navigating the Challenges of Remote and Distributed Team Management:

In the aftermath of the COVID-19 pandemic, remote work became a reality for countless organizations. This shift presented distinct challenges and opportunities for product teams. To successfully navigate these challenges, consider the following:

Communication Hurdles: The abrupt transition to remote work accentuated communication obstacles. Differences in time zones, language barriers, and technology issues became more pronounced. Addressing these challenges required the establishment of clear communication protocols and enhanced language support.

Isolation and Burnout: The blurring of boundaries between work and personal life led to feelings of isolation and burnout among team members. Counteracting these effects demanded the encouragement of regular breaks, the setting of boundaries, and a commitment to promoting work-life balance.

Cultural and Time Zone Differences: Remote teams, now more than ever, spanned diverse cultures and time zones. Sensitivity to cultural nuances and flexibility in scheduling became even more vital for maintaining teamwork.

Accountability and Productivity: Ensuring that team members remained accountable and productive in a remote setup was of paramount importance. To achieve this, it was essential to define clear expectations, set realistic goals, and implement productivity tracking tools.

Team Building: Building a sense of camaraderie and teamwork within remote teams was a priority in post-COVID-19 world. Organizing virtual team-building activities and encouraging team members to connect on a personal level despite physical distance was a valuable practice.

Tools and Technologies for Efficient Remote Collaboration:

In the wake of the pandemic, various tools and technologies continued to play a pivotal role in ensuring efficient collaboration among remote teams:

Communication Platforms: Tools like Slack, Microsoft Teams, or Zoom retained their significance in facilitating real-time communication among remote teams.

Project Management Software: Remote project management tools such as Trello, Asana, or Jira remained essential for tracking project progress and fostering collaboration.

File Sharing and Cloud Storage: Secure and accessible file sharing through platforms like Google Drive or Dropbox continued to be the norm in remote work scenarios.

Virtual Whiteboards: Virtual whiteboard applications like Miro or Microsoft Whiteboard remained invaluable for collaborative brainstorming and planning.

Security Measures: In the post-COVID-19 remote work landscape, cybersecurity measures to protect sensitive data gained even greater importance.

Building Trust and Maintaining Cohesion in Virtual Teams:

The post-pandemic world emphasized the continued need to build trust and cohesion within remote teams:

Clear Expectations: Clarity in roles, responsibilities, and expectations was pivotal in building trust within remote teams.

Regular Check-Ins: Scheduled one-on-one and team check-ins remained a core component of maintaining open lines of communication in remote work scenarios.

Team Culture: Cultivating a strong team culture that transcended physical locations continued to be a cornerstone. Celebrating achievements, acknowledging milestones, and supporting one another were essential for maintaining cohesion.

Feedback and Recognition: Offering constructive feedback and recognition for a job well done remained a key element in building trust and fostering unity.

Transparency: In the post-COVID-19 remote work landscape, transparency in decision-making processes and project updates held even greater value, fostering trust and unity.

The COVID-19 pandemic reshaped the way we work and made remote work a reality for countless organizations. It demonstrated that, when managed effectively, remote, and distributed teams can be transformative, offering global talent access and enhanced flexibility. In the chapters that follow, we'll continue exploring how to nurture innovation and excellence in this ever-changing landscape.

Evaluating and Developing Team Members

This section focuses on employing performance assessment methodologies, offering constructive feedback, and creating a culture of continuous learning and development within the team. Just like the North Star guiding a ship, these principles serve as your compass in navigating the path of leadership.

Performance assessment methodologies are your guiding compass to steer your team in the right direction:

1. Key Performance Indicators (KPIs): These metrics align with your product's goals and reveal how each team member contributes to your product's success.
2. 360-Degree Feedback: Feedback from all directions helps identify strengths and areas for improvement.
3. Self-Assessments: Encourage team members to assess their performance and set personal goals.
4. Objective Key Results (OKRs): These objectives guide their

focus and measure their impact on the team's success.
5. Regular Check-Ins: One-on-one meetings provide a platform for open communication regarding performance.

Offering feedback is like steering your team towards growth:

1. Specific Feedback: It's precise and actionable.
2. Goal Alignment: Individual goals align with broader team objectives.
3. Feedback Loops: Continuous exchange of ideas and suggestions fosters a culture of growth.
4. Recognition and Appreciation: Recognize and appreciate team members' efforts and achievements.
5. Constructive Criticism: Emphasize potential solutions and growth opportunities.

Foster a culture of continuous learning and development:

1. Training and Workshops: Enhance skills and knowledge through training programs and workshops.
2. Mentorship: Experienced team members guide and mentor newcomers.
3. Cross-Functional Collaboration: Encourage exposure to different aspects of product management.
4. Innovation Time: Dedicate time for innovative projects and experimentation.
5. Recognition of Expertise: Acknowledge team members who become experts in specific domains.

As you navigate through performance assessments, feedback, and continuous learning, you'll witness the development of a high-performing team that propels your product towards remarkable success.

8 INNOVATION CULTURE

Innovation needs structure to thrive. Innovation needs structure to thrive; this is a principle that lies at the heart of successful product management. While spontaneity and creative thinking have their place, the realm of excellence in product development is not one where 'Jugaad,' or makeshift solutions, holds any sway. In this chapter, we delve into the intricate yet crucial world of structured innovation and how it can drive product management efforts to unprecedented heights.

Innovation is the compass that guides product managers through the ever-changing landscape of customer needs and market dynamics. It's the driving force behind new features, improved user experiences, and staying ahead of the competition. However, like any endeavor, innovation requires a structured approach to ensure that it contributes to, rather than hinders, the pursuit of excellence.

So, what does it mean to innovate with structure? this means adopting methodologies, frameworks, and strategies that not only stimulate creativity but also provide a clear path toward achievable, valuable results. This means recognizing that innovation is not a mere flash of genius but a process that can be cultivated and optimized.

In this chapter, we explore the intricacies of structured innovation, covering a various tools, techniques, and frameworks that can help you and your product team thrive in the pursuit of excellence. From design thinking to agile development, from user-centric design to rapid prototyping, we will navigate this multifaceted realm with the goal of fostering a culture of innovation where every idea is worth exploring but only the best ideas are worth pursuing.

Essence of Structured Innovation

They provide roadmap for turning concepts into tangible solutions and products.

Design Thinking: Design thinking, often referred to as the compass of user-centric innovation, encourages product managers to put themselves in the shoes of their end-users. By empathizing with user's needs and challenges, you can identify opportunities for meaningful innovation. The design thinking process typically involves stages such as empathizing, defining, ideating, prototyping, and testing.

Exercise: Design Thinking Challenge

Background: You are a product manager tasked with improving the user experience of a mobile banking app. Your goal is to make it more user-friendly, intuitive, and appealing to various customers. You've decided to apply design thinking principles to tackle this challenge.

Scenario: Your team has gathered for a design thinking workshop. In this exercise, you will go through the stages of design thinking to address specific issues with the mobile banking app. Your task is to develop innovative solutions that enhance the user experience.

Instructions:

1. Empathize (60 minutes): Begin by understanding the users' pain points and needs. Each team member should interview at least two potential users or stakeholders. Ask them about their experiences with the current app, what problems they've encountered, and what features they'd like to see improved.

2. Define (30 minutes): Share insights from your interviews. Identify common themes and create a user persona representing a typical app user. Define a specific problem statement that

encapsulates the main issue to be addressed.

3. Ideate (45 minutes): Generate as many ideas as possible to solve the defined problem. Encourage wild, out-of-the-box thinking. Use techniques such as brainstorming, mind mapping, or 'how might we' questions that spark creativity. Write each idea on a sticky note.

4. Prototype (60 minutes): Choose the most promising ideas from the ideation phase and create simple, low-fidelity prototypes for each. These can be sketches, wireframes, or paper prototypes. The goal is to have a visual representation of your ideas.

5. Test (45 minutes): Present your prototypes to a small group of users (colleagues or friends). Gather feedback on the new concepts. Take note of their reactions, comments, and suggestions.

6. Reflect (30 minutes): Reconvene as a team to discuss feedback from users. Reflect on what worked well and what didn't. Identify any insights gained from this exercise.

Presentation: Each team will have 10 minutes to present their problem statement, the selected idea, and the prototype to the entire group. Be prepared to explain the rationale behind your design thinking choices.

Debrief: Conclude the exercise with a debriefing session. Discuss the challenges faced during each stage of the design thinking process and how this approach can drive innovation in product management.

This exercise encourages you to think creatively, understand the user's perspective, and prototype solutions before implementing changes to the app. It's a practical application of design thinking principles that can lead to meaningful improvements in the user experience of mobile banking apps.

Agile Development: Agile methodologies, such as Scrum and Kanban, offer the ship that carries your product through the seas of iterative development. These processes allow for incremental, customer-driven improvements. Short development cycles, called sprints, keep your product's journey on a steady course toward meeting user needs and market demands.

Exercise: The Agile Development Challenge

Background: You are a product manager leading a cross-functional team responsible for developing project management software. The team has faced challenges with project prioritization, task tracking, and user feedback incorporation. To address these issues, you've decided to conduct an Agile development exercise.

Scenario: Your team has gathered for an Agile development workshop. In this exercise, you will go through the Agile process to improve your project management software. Your goal is to become more agile, increase flexibility, and enhance the team collaboration.

Instructions:

1. Sprint Planning (30 minutes): Begin by identifying a specific feature or improvement for the project management software. The team should discuss and prioritize this feature. Define the user stories and tasks that need to be completed during the sprint.

2. Sprint Execution (60 minutes): Allocate 60 minutes to execute your sprint. Team members should work on their assigned tasks, making incremental progress toward the feature's completion. Use Agile tools such as a physical or digital board to track task status.

3. Daily Stand-up (15 minutes): Hold a daily stand-up meeting to discuss progress, challenges, and potential roadblocks. Each team member should answer three questions: What have you accomplished since the last stand-up? What are you planning to do next? Are there any obstacles in your way?

4. Sprint Review (30 minutes): At the end of the sprint, conduct a review meeting. Demonstrate the completed feature or improvements to the team. Discuss what went well and what

could be improved. Use the feedback to adjust your development process.

5. Sprint Retrospective (30 minutes): Reflect on the sprint as a team. Discuss what aspects of your Agile process worked and what didn't. Identify opportunities for improvement and plan actions to enhance the next sprint.

Presentation: Each team will have 10 minutes to present their sprint results to the entire group. Explain the features or improvements developed during the sprint, the challenges faced, and the team's retrospective findings.

Debrief: Conclude the exercise with a debriefing session. Discuss the effectiveness of Agile methodologies, the challenges encountered during the exercise, and how adopting Agile can improve the team's efficiency and product development process.

This exercise provides hands-on experience of Agile development, emphasizing the importance of iterative progress, daily collaboration, and the value of sprint reviews and retrospectives. It helps you understand the benefits of Agile methodologies and how they can enhance your product management process.

Rapid Prototyping: Prototyping is an island of experimentation, where ideas can be tested and refined. Rapid prototyping tools and practices empower product teams to create and assess early versions of a product or feature, thereby gathering valuable user feedback to guide future iterations.

Exercise: The Rapid Prototyping Challenge

Background: As a product manager, you're faced with the task of creating a more user-friendly interface for an e-commerce website. To achieve this, you've decided to conduct a rapid prototyping exercise with your team.

Scenario: Your team has assembled for a rapid prototyping workshop. In this exercise, you will go through the steps of rapid prototyping to address user interface challenges. Your goal is to quickly create and test prototypes to improve the website's usability.

Instructions:

1. Identify the problem (15 minutes): Start by identifying a specific aspect of the e-commerce website's interface that needs improvement. This could be related to navigation, product search, or checkout. Clearly define the problem you want to address.

2. Ideation (30 minutes): Encourage the team to brainstorm and generate ideas for improving the identified interface aspect. No idea is too wild at this stage. Write these ideas on sticky notes.

3. Prototyping (45 minutes): Select one or more of the most promising ideas from the ideation phase. Create low-fidelity paper prototypes or digital wireframes representing potential solutions to the problem. Keep the prototypes simple and clear.

4. User testing (30 minutes): Enlist a few team members or colleagues to act as users. Have them interact with the prototypes and provide feedback. Observe their reactions and ask for their thoughts and suggestions.

5. Iterate (30 minutes): Based on user feedback, make necessary adjustments to the prototypes. You might need to create new versions or revise existing ones. The goal is to refine the prototypes based on user insights.

6. Presentation (15 minutes): Each team will have 10 minutes to present their prototype, explaining the problem they addressed, the prototype solution, and the changes made based on user feedback.

Debrief: Conclude the exercise with a debriefing session. Discuss the effectiveness of rapid prototyping, the challenges faced during the exercise, and how adopting this approach can lead to more user-friendly interfaces in product development.

This exercise allows you to experience the benefits of rapid prototyping in real-time. It emphasizes the importance of quick and iterative design improvements based on user feedback, which can be a game-changer in enhancing the usability of your e-commerce website.

User-Centric Design: User-centric design keeps the user experience at the forefront of product development. By studying and understanding your users, you can craft features and interfaces that resonate with them. This approach ensures that your product's voyage leads to increased user satisfaction and loyalty.

Exercise: The User-Centric Design Challenge

Background: You're a product manager tasked with enhancing the user experience of a social networking app. To address this challenge effectively, you've decided to conduct a User-Centric Design exercise with your team.

Scenario: Your team has gathered for a User-Centric Design workshop. In this exercise, you will focus on understanding user needs, developing user-centric solutions, and creating prototypes to improve the social networking app's user experience.

Instructions:

1. User Research (45 minutes): Start by understanding your users. Each team member should conduct user research by interviewing a current or potential user of the social networking app. Ask questions about their usage patterns, pain points, and what features they'd like to see improved.

2. Persona Creation (30 minutes): Share insights from user interviews. Identify common themes and create user personas based on your findings. These personas represent typical users of the app.

3. Ideation (30 minutes): Encourage the team to brainstorm and generate ideas for improving the user experience based on user personas. What features, changes, or enhancements would

address their needs and challenges? Capture these ideas on sticky notes.

4. Wireframing (45 minutes): Select one or more of the most promising ideas from the ideation phase. Create wireframes or sketches that visualize potential solutions. Keep the wireframes simple but clear in conveying the user-centric improvements.

5. User testing (30 minutes): Enlist a few team members or colleagues to act as users. Have them interact with the wireframes and provide feedback. Observe their reactions and ask for their thoughts and suggestions.

6. Prototype (45 minutes): Based on user feedback, make necessary adjustments to the wireframes, and create interactive digital prototypes. The goal is to have a working model of user-centric improvements.

7. Presentation (15 minutes): Each team will have 10 minutes to present their user-centric design, explaining the user research, personas created, the ideation process, wireframes, and the user-centric improvements based on feedback.

Debrief: Conclude the exercise with a debriefing session. Discuss the effectiveness of user-centric design, the challenges faced during the exercise, and how adopting this approach can lead to substantial enhancements in the user experience of the social networking app.

This exercise provides a hands-on experience of user-centric design principles. It emphasizes the importance of understanding users' needs, ideating solutions that align with those needs, and testing those solutions to create an app that truly resonates with the user base.

Innovative Frameworks for Success

Structured innovation involves not only adopting methodologies but also embracing innovation frameworks that shape and guide your product management efforts. Some of these frameworks include:

Lean Startup

Lean Startup principles have reshaped the landscape of product management, emphasizing a dynamic and efficient approach to building, and launching products. This methodology urges product managers to embrace a more experimental and customer-centric mindset. In this section, we will delve into the core principles of the Lean Startup approach and explore how they can guide your product management journey.

Core Principles of Lean Startup

1. Build-Measure-Learn: The foundation of Lean Startup is the iterative Build-Measure-Learn cycle. Instead of aiming for a perfect, all-encompassing product from the start, build a minimum viable product (MVP) to test your core hypotheses. You then measure its performance and gather user feedback to learn what works and what doesn't. This cycle helps you refine and adapt your product based on real-world insights.

2. Validated Learning: Lean Startup encourages a focus on validated learning. Instead of making assumptions about what customers want, you actively seek to validate those assumptions through experimentation. This data-driven approach minimizes the risk of building features or products that won't resonate with your target audience.

3. Pivot or Persevere: A key tenet of Lean Startup is the willingness to pivot or persevere. If your MVP reveals that your initial idea isn't gaining traction, you can pivot by adjusting your strategy or trying a new direction. Conversely, if you see positive feedback and traction, you persevere by optimizing and expanding on your current path.

4. Continuous Deployment: Lean Startup embraces continuous deployment, which means that you deploy product changes or updates frequently, often daily or weekly. This approach ensures that you can respond quickly to user feedback, make improvements, and pivot as necessary.

Practical Application of the Lean Startup

1. Hypothesis Testing: In your product management journey, you'll regularly develop hypotheses about what your users want or need. Lean Startup encourages you to turn these hypotheses into experiments by building MVPs to validate or invalidate them.

2. A/B Testing: A/B testing is a common practice in Lean Startup. You test two or more versions of a feature or webpage with slight variations to determine which one performs better. This allows you to make data-informed decisions about what resonates with users.

3. Metrics-Driven Decision Making: Lean Startup emphasizes metrics as the compass for product management. You define key performance indicators (KPIs) and track them rigorously. Whether it's conversion rates, user engagement, or retention, these metrics guide your decision-making process.

4. Minimum Viable Product (MVP): MVP is a fundamental concept in Lean Startup. It's the simplest version of your product that allows you to start the Build-Measure-Learn cycle. By releasing an MVP, you gather crucial feedback and adapt your product based on real user experiences.

Lean Startup principles provide a structured and practical approach to product management. By embracing the core tenets of experimentation, validated learning, and data-driven decision-making, you can navigate the complex product development journey with greater confidence and efficiency. Lean Startup is not only a methodology but a mindset shift that encourages continuous improvement and adaptability, which are essential in the ever-evolving world of product management.

Exercise: Applying Lean Startup Principles

Background: You manage a team responsible for developing a fitness and wellness app. You're committed to ensuring that the app truly resonates with users and addresses their needs. In this exercise, you'll apply Lean Startup principles to refine a specific feature of the app.

Scenario: You've identified a feature in your fitness app that could use improvement – the meal planning section. Users have provided mixed feedback about its usability and effectiveness. Your goal is to leverage Lean Startup principles to enhance this feature.

Instructions:

1. Define the problem (15 minutes): Start by defining the problem. What specific issues have users encountered with the meal planning feature? Is it a lack of relevant recipes, complicated navigation, or insufficient personalization? Write a clear problem statement.

2. Hypothesis Formulation (20 minutes): Develop a hypothesis about how to address the identified problem. For example, "We believe that by providing more personalized meal plans based on dietary preferences, we can improve user satisfaction with the meal planning feature."

3. Build an MVP (45 minutes): Develop an MVP that reflects your hypothesis. In this case, it might be a simplified version of the meal planning feature with enhanced personalization. This might include dietary options, a recipe recommendation engine, and a user-friendly interface.

4. A/B Testing (30 minutes): Set up an A/B test to compare the new MVP with the existing meal planning feature. Define metrics to track, such as user engagement with the new feature, recipe adoption, and user satisfaction scores.

5. User Feedback Collection (60 minutes): Deploy the A/B test to a sample of app users. After a set period, collect user feedback through surveys, in-app feedback forms, or direct interviews. Ask users about their experience with the new feature and any suggestions for improvement.

6. Data Analysis (30 minutes): Analyze the data from the A/B test and user feedback. Determine whether the MVP led to better

user engagement and satisfaction. Did it address the identified problem effectively?

7. Pivot or Persevere (20 minutes): Based on the data and user feedback, decide. If the MVP yielded positive results, consider incorporating these changes into the full meal planning feature. If not, pivot by redefining your hypothesis and MVP.

Presentation: Each team will have 10 minutes to present their problem statement, hypothesis, MVP, A/B test results, and their decision to pivot or persevere.

Examples: Here are some examples of Lean Startup principles in action:

- A/B testing of the impact of a redesigned homepage on user click-through rates.

- Creating an MVP for a mobile app with basic functionality to test the concept before building a full-featured app.

- Running a series of email marketing campaigns with different subject lines and measuring open rates to identify the most effective approach.

This exercise enables you to experience Lean Startup principles firsthand by addressing a specific problem in your fitness and wellness app. It emphasizes iterative development, validated learning, and data-driven decision-making, which are fundamental aspects of the Lean Startup methodology.

Innovation Sprints

Innovation sprints, often referred to as design sprints or ideation sprints, are a dynamic and focused approach to problem-solving that fosters creative thinking and rapid idea generation. In this section, we'll explore the concept of innovation sprints and how they can be a valuable tool in your product management toolkit.

What are innovation sprints?

Innovation sprints are structured, time-bound workshops aimed at generating innovative solutions to specific challenges. They draw inspiration from various design thinking and creative problem-solving methodologies. The key characteristics of innovation sprints include:

1. Cross-Functional Collaboration: Innovation sprints bring together team members from diverse backgrounds, including product managers, designers, engineers, and marketers. This cross-functional collaboration ensures several perspectives and expertise.

2. Time-Limited: Innovation sprints are typically short and intense, often spanning a few days to a week. The compressed timeframe encourages focused effort and prevents overthinking.

3. Clear Problem Definition: The sprint begins with a clear definition of the problem or challenge that requires innovative solutions. This problem statement serves as the foundation for the entire sprint.

4. Structured Process: The sprint follows a structured process that typically includes stages for ideation, solution sketching, prototyping, and testing. Each stage has a specific time allocation and set of activities.

5. User-centric: Throughout the sprint, the user remains at the center of the process. All solutions and ideas are evaluated on the basis of their potential to address user needs and pain points.

Practical Application of Innovation Sprints

1. Problem Framing (1 day): Start with a problem-framing session, in which the team collectively defines and understands the challenge. The goal is to ensure that everyone has a shared understanding of what needs to be addressed.

2. Ideation (1-2 days): Encourage team members to brainstorm and ideate potential solutions without judgment. Use techniques such

as brainwriting, mind mapping, and the "Crazy 8s" exercise to generate a broad range of ideas.

3. Solution Sketching (1 day): Have team members individually sketch their proposed solutions. These sketches can range from rough drawings to flowcharts, that illustrate how the solutions might work.

4. Prototyping (1-2 days): Based on the sketches, create simple prototypes or mockups of the most promising solutions. These prototypes should be quick and low fidelity, focusing on core functionality.

5. User Testing (1 day): Test the prototypes with real users or stakeholders. Gather feedback on the usability, desirability, and effectiveness of the solutions.

6. Decision and Next Steps (1 day): After user testing, the team collectively decides which solution or combination of solutions to pursue. Create a roadmap for implementation and further development.

Examples of Innovation Sprints:

1. Improving E-commerce Checkout: An e-commerce company conducts an innovation sprint to streamline its checkout process, resulting in a more user-friendly and efficient design that reduces cart abandonment rates.

2. Enhancing Mobile App Onboarding: A mobile app developer uses an innovation sprint to reconfigure its boarding process, resulting in a more engaging and intuitive experience for new users.

3. Content Recommendation Algorithm: A media streaming service organizes an innovation sprint to brainstorm ways to enhance its content recommendation algorithm, leading to a more personalized and accurate system.

Innovation sprints are a powerful approach for tackling complex problems and fostering creativity within your product team. By embracing these structured, time-limited workshops, you can accelerate idea generation, encourage cross-functional collaboration, and drive innovation in your product management efforts.

Building a Culture of Experimentation and Learning

Innovation is not a linear path; it's a landscape marked with twists, turns, and occasional setbacks. To foster innovation effectively, embracing experimentation is key. In this section, we'll explore strategies for nurturing a culture of experimentation and learning within your product management team.

1. Fail Forward:

Embrace the notion of "failing forward." In the world of innovation, failure is not a roadblock but a steppingstone. Encourage your team to view failures as valuable learning experiences. Each attempt, even if it doesn't yield the desired outcome, contributes to the refinement of ideas and strategies. Through these failures, innovative solutions often emerge. Share stories of famous innovations that arise from initial setbacks to inspire your team.

2. Learning from Mistakes:

Cultivate a culture where mistakes are seen as opportunities for growth. When a mistake occurs, rather than assigning blame, focus on understanding what went wrong and why. Encourage team members to analyze these failures, extract valuable lessons, and apply those lessons to future endeavors. Share instances when identifying and rectifying mistakes led to significant improvements, fostering a culture that embraces constructive criticism.

3. Experimentation Mindset:

Foster an experimentation mindset within your team. Encourage team members to test hypotheses, gather data, and adapt their strategies based on the results. This mindset should extend to all aspects of product management, from user experience design to marketing tactics. Designate specific periods or initiatives for experimentation and innovation. Highlight successful experiments and showcase how they contributed to product evolution.

4. Knowledge Sharing:

Create platforms and mechanisms for knowledge sharing. Innovative ideas and practices can come from any team member. Encourage open and transparent communication, where insights, findings, and innovative practices are readily shared with colleagues. Consider hosting regular "innovation forums" or knowledge-sharing sessions where team members can present their experiments, discuss their results, and offer feedback to one another.

5. Continuous Improvement:

Emphasize the importance of continuous improvement. Encourage your team members to identify areas for enhancement, both within their individual roles and in the broader product management process. Use techniques such as retrospectives or feedback loops to regularly assess what's working and what's not. By involving the entire team in the improvement process, you can continuously refine and optimize your product management practices.

Examples of an Embracing Experimentation:

1. A/B Testing for Email Campaigns: A marketing team regularly conducts A/B tests on email campaigns, experimenting with different subject lines, content, and send times. Failures in some tests provide insights into what doesn't resonate with the audience, leading to more successful campaigns.

2. User-Centered Design Iterations: During the development of a mobile app, the design team engages in iterative testing with real users. Their willingness to experiment with different user interfaces and features allows them to create an app that better aligns with user preferences.

3. Agile Development Practices: A product development team follows Agile practices, including sprint retrospectives. In these retrospectives, they discuss what went well and what didn't

during the sprint, enabling continuous improvements in the development process.

By infusing your product management journey with a culture of experimentation, you'll empower your team to take calculated risks, learn from failures, and adapt quickly. Innovation becomes a dynamic, ever-evolving process, where each experiment contributes to the growth and evolution of your products.

9 AI/ML PRODUCT MANAGEMENT

Our previous explorations of product management have provided us with invaluable insights and strategies that form the foundation of this chapter. We've learned about identifying opportunities, defining product strategies, building cross-functional teams, and the significance of user-centric design. In this chapter, we're applying these principles to the dynamic and transformative world of AI/ML product management.

As we delve into the AI/ML landscape, we'll uncover the unique challenges and opportunities that product managers encounter when working with cutting-edge technologies. From data acquisition and management to ethical considerations and regulatory compliance, we'll navigate this landscape with curiosity and a commitment to excellence.

Through case studies, real-world examples, and practical strategies, we'll unveil the art of product management in the context of AI/ML, providing you with the tools and knowledge needed to excel in this exciting and rapidly advancing field.

So, whether you're a seasoned product manager looking to expand your skill set or a newcomer eager to understand the synergy between AI/ML and product management, let's explore this together, ready to embrace the future and the endless possibilities it holds.

Introduction to AI/ML in Product Management

Artificial Intelligence and Machine Learning, commonly referred to as AI/ML, have revolutionized industries, from healthcare to finance, and are now an integral part of the technological landscape. To excel in AI/ML product management, it's essential to grasp the fundamental aspects of this dynamic field.

AI vs. ML: Artificial Intelligence encompasses the broader concept of creating machines or systems capable of performing tasks that typically require human intelligence. Machine Learning is a subset of AI that enables machines to learn from data and improve their performance without being explicitly programed.

GenAI: GenAI, short for Generative Artificial Intelligence, refers to a category of artificial intelligence systems designed to generate content that is often creative, original, and data driven. These systems can create new data or content, such as images, text, audio, or even videos, on the basis of patterns and examples they have learned from existing data.

AI/ML Use Cases: AI/ML has found applications in various domains. For instance, in healthcare, it aids in disease diagnosis, whereas in e-commerce, it personalizes recommendations for users. Understanding these applications is vital for product managers to identify potential opportunities.

Data-Driven Decisions: AI/ML heavily relies on data. The more data you have, the better the model's performance. As a product manager, you must understand how data collection, storage, and processing impact your product.

AI/ML Algorithms: There's a multitude of AI/ML algorithms, each suited to specific tasks. Knowledge of these algorithms and their applications is invaluable for product managers.

AI/ML Challenges: AI/ML introduces unique challenges. These include ensuring data privacy, addressing bias in algorithms, and navigating regulatory requirements. Awareness of these challenges is crucial for effective product management.

AI/ML Trends: AI/ML is a rapidly evolving field. Stay up to date with the latest trends, from advances in Natural Language Processing to breakthroughs in computer vision. This knowledge helps you make informed decisions about your AI/ML product strategy.

User-centric AI/ML: Finally, remember that AI/ML products are built for users. Understanding user needs and expectations in the context of AI/ML is paramount.

By comprehending these foundational aspects, product managers will be better prepared to take on the challenges and opportunities that presented by AI/ML.

Product managers play a pivotal role in AI/ML by ensuring that these cutting-edge technologies not only meet real-world needs but also adhere to ethical standards and regulatory requirements. In the evolving landscape of AI/ML, where technology can inadvertently introduce biases and privacy concerns, product managers become the guiding ethical force. Their responsibility extends to guaranteeing that AI/ML products are ethically developed and used, promoting unbiased decision-making, and preserving user privacy.

AI/ML operates within a legal framework that is in a constant state of flux. Regulations in this domain evolve to address new challenges and ensure ethical and responsible use. Therefore, product managers must navigate this ever-changing regulatory landscape, ensuring that their products comply with data protection laws and industry-specific guidelines.

In the vast expanse of AI/ML, product managers play the vital role of ethical guardians and regulatory navigators. Their dedication to upholding the highest ethical and legal standards ensures that AI/ML technologies are not only groundbreaking but also trustworthy and aligned with societal values. They safeguard user trust and the ethical use of AI/ML innovations.

Identifying Opportunities

Product managers play a central role in recognizing avenues for innovation and aligning these opportunities with the needs of the market and the expectations of customers. In this section, we discuss the significance of data-driven insights, best practices, and examples that highlight their practical application in AI/ML product management.

Data-driven insights are transformative for product innovation in AI/ML. They offer a systematic, evidence-based approach to understanding user behavior, trends, and patterns. These insights guide decision-making, enabling product managers to make informed choices that drive product success.

Best Practices for Data-Driven Product Innovation:

1. Establish Clear Objectives: Define clear objectives for data analysis. Determine what specific questions you answer or problems to solve through data insights.

2. Collect Comprehensive Data: Gather several data sources, from user interactions to system performance metrics. A diverse dataset provides a more holistic understanding of your product's performance.

3. Use Advanced Analytics: Employ advanced analytics techniques, including machine learning and predictive modeling, to extract valuable insights from complex datasets.

4. Iterate and Experiment: Continuously iterate and experiment with data analysis. Explore different variables and metrics to obtain unexpected insights.

5. User-Centric Focus: Always keep the user at the center of your analysis. Understand user behavior, preferences, and pain points to shape user-centric product innovations.

Practical Examples:

• Personalization in Content Recommendations: AI-driven platforms such as Netflix and Spotify analyze user viewing or listening history to provide personalized content recommendations. By leveraging data-driven insights, they enhance user experience and drive engagement.

• Predictive Maintenance in Manufacturing: AI-driven predictive maintenance solutions analyze machine data to predict when equipment is likely to fail. This minimizes downtime and reduces maintenance costs, leading to improved operational efficiency.

- Healthcare Diagnosis Support: AI systems analyze patient data to assist medical professionals in diagnosing diseases. By using data-driven insights, these systems enhance diagnostic accuracy and treatment planning.

Product managers must embrace a data-centric approach, using advanced analytics and a user-centric focus to continuously improve and enhance their products. By doing so, they can create solutions that not only meet but also exceed user expectations.

Market analysis and understanding of customer needs are integral components of AI/ML product management. Market analysis equips product managers with insights into the competitive landscape, industry trends, and emerging technologies in AI/ML. Simultaneously, understanding customer needs ensures that product development aligns with real-world requirements. These two facets are crucial for identifying opportunities and driving innovation.

Best practices for market analysis and customer needs:

1. Comprehensive Market Research: Conduct thorough market research to understand industry dynamics, competitor strategies, and emerging AI/ML technologies. Stay updated on market trends and disruptions.

2. Customer-Centric Approach: Prioritize the voice of the customer. Engage in surveys, interviews, and user research to gain profound insights into customer needs, pain points, and expectations.

3. Segmentation: Segment your market to identify specific user groups with distinct needs. Tailor product offerings to address these segments effectively.

4. Competitor Analysis: Analyze competitors to identify gaps in their offerings. Leverage this knowledge to develop distinctive AI/ML products that meet unmet needs.

5. Continuous Feedback Loop: Establish a feedback loop with customers and users. Regularly solicit feedback and iteratively enhance the product to align with evolving needs.

Practical Examples:

- Voice Assistants: Companies such as Amazon with Alexa and Apple with Siri conducted extensive market research to understand the growing trend of voice-activated AI. They recognized the need for a user-friendly interface and delivered products that seamlessly integrated into users' lives.

- Healthcare Diagnostics: AI-driven solutions in healthcare, like IBM's Watson, integrate market insights and customer needs. These solutions offer advanced diagnostics and decision support to healthcare professionals, addressing the industry's demand for improved patient care.

- E-commerce Recommendations: AI/ML-powered product recommendation engines on platforms such as Amazon and Netflix analyze user behavior and preferences. These recommendations align with customer needs for personalized and relevant content.

Defining the AI/ML Product Strategy

In this section, we explore the art of defining a robust AI/ML product strategy, which involves setting clear objectives and key results (OKRs) and striking a balance between business goals and technical capabilities.

Objective and Key Result (OKR) frameworks offer a systematic way to define and assess the success of a product. This is particularly crucial in the realm of AI/ML product management. However, we won't delve into the OKR specifics here, as you can refer to the previous chapters for that. Instead, we'll emphasize the importance of finding the right equilibrium for a prosperous AI/ML product strategy. In the AI/ML landscape, product managers frequently encounter the intersection of technological potential and business ambitions.

Finding the equilibrium:

Business Alignment: Product managers function as the vital link between business leaders and technical teams. They are entrusted with the responsibility of harmonizing the AI/ML product with broader business objectives. This entails:

- Understanding Business Strategy: Product managers delve into the core of business strategy. They acquire a profound understanding of the overarching goals, revenue targets, market positioning, and customer expectations.

- Ensuring Alignment: With insights into the business strategy, product managers ensure that the AI/ML product is tightly aligned with these objectives. They set clear expectations, ensuring that the product contributes to the organization's overarching mission.

Technical Feasibility: The capabilities and limitations of AI/ML technology play a significant role in shaping product strategy. Product managers engage closely with data scientists and engineers to gauge what is feasible within technological boundaries. This involves:

- Technology Assessment: Product managers team up with tech experts to select the best tools for AI and ML. They explore high-tech stuff like machine learning frameworks (think TensorFlow, PyTorch and Ray) and data processing tools (like Apache Spark and Hadoop) to crunch big data. In special AI areas like Natural Language Processing (NLP) and Computer Vision libraries such as NLTK and OpenCV are used for language and image magic. Storing data safely in databases (say, MongoDB) and infrastructure selection using cloud platforms (such as AWS or GCP) or on-prem (such as HPE GreenLake) is key. To label data and simplify machine learning, tools like Labelbox and AutoML platforms (e.g., Google AutoML) come into play. When it's time to launch, they deploy models using tools like Docker (or KServe) and keep a watchful eye with MLflow and TensorBoard. This smart tool selection ensures that AI/ML projects run smoothly and meet their goals.

- Determining Boundaries: Understanding the boundaries of AI/ML technology is crucial. First, product managers must assess and ensure data quality, recognizing that poor input data can lead to inaccurate results. They also considered the limits of computational resources, balancing available computing power, and associated costs. In addition, they acknowledge algorithmic boundaries and constraints, determining where AI and ML can excel and where their limitations lie. Moreover, they adhere to rules and regulations specific to their industry, ensuring legal compliance, and navigate deployment constraints to seamlessly integrate AI models into existing systems.

- Risk Assessment and Mitigation: Product managers take the lead in identifying potential pitfalls, like model biases, data security vulnerabilities, and ethical concerns, diligently gauging their impact on the product's ultimate success. Once these risks are identified, product managers move ahead with mitigation strategies. These strategies may involve bolstering data security protocols to guard against vulnerabilities, applying bias-reduction techniques for equitable outcomes, and ensuring unwavering compliance with industry regulations. Think of this process as a guided path where product managers act as seasoned guides, skillfully charting a course that recognizes and addresses risks, ensuring a smoother path through the terrain of AI/ML.

Iterative Approach: AI/ML products often require an iterative approach due to the evolving nature of technology and user expectations. Product managers continuously assess progress and adapt the product strategy to ensure alignment with both business and technical considerations. This includes:

- Continuous Evaluation: Product managers regularly evaluate the product's performance against predefined metrics. They gather user feedback and monitor key performance indicators to assess the product's impact.

- Adaptive Strategy: In response to changing dynamics, product managers adapt the strategy. They may pivot the product direction, enhance features, or address emerging challenges to ensure that the product remains aligned with the ever-evolving landscape.

Data Acquisition and Management

In the world of AI/ML, data play a pivotal role in product development. Product managers lead the way in collecting and overseeing this critical resource, overseeing a series of tasks to ensure data's quality, privacy, and security.

Gathering and processing data for AI/ML products

Product managers initiate the process of data acquisition by identifying the AI/ML product's specific data needs. They work closely with data engineers and scientists to pinpoint relevant datasets from various sources, including internal databases, external providers, and user-generated data.

After identifying the pertinent datasets, product managers collaborate with data engineers to securely collect and store the data. They follow DataOps practices, employing version control systems like Git, DVC and utilizing cloud-based storage solutions, such as AWS S3 or Google Cloud Storage, for scalable and secure data repositories. These tools help in data organization and in maintaining a historical record of changes.

Data transformation is the stage in which raw data is refined into a format suitable for AI model consumption. Product managers, in coordination with data engineers and data scientists, utilize data processing tools like Apache Spark and Pandas for data cleaning, feature engineering, and data preparation. This step is similar to piecing together a complex puzzle, where each data point forms a part of the larger picture.

Throughout the process, DataOps practices are seamlessly integrated. Product managers oversee the implementation of DataOps tools like Prefect for workflow management and data monitoring solutions like DataDog, which track data quality, lineage, and pipeline orchestration. These tools ensure that data are continually refreshed and updated to maintain the AI/ML product's accuracy.

Ensuring Data Privacy and Security

In the ever-evolving field of AI and ML, product managers take on the pivotal responsibility of not only accumulating extensive data but also ensuring the safeguarding of this invaluable asset. In today's digital age, data has attained the status of a precious resource, heightening the imperative to protect it. Product managers, much like vigilant protectors, are entrusted with the meticulous preservation of data privacy and security, manifesting these principles as they navigate consequential decisions.

Imagine your AI/ML project as a sanctuary, with data at its core— an asset to be protected. Here's a practical approach to strengthening data security:

Access Control: Similar to sentinels guarding a stronghold, implement stringent access controls to limit data access to authorized personnel. Use identity and access management tools to enforce these controls.

Encryption: Employ encryption techniques for data, both in transit and at rest, using industry standards like Advanced Encryption Standards (AES) to ensure data security.

Data Masking: Think of data masking as providing a disguise to sensitive information within the data. It conceals portions of data to protect sensitive details, such as credit card numbers in a database.

Regular Audits: Conduct periodic security audits to identify vulnerabilities and areas that require reinforcement, like regular security inspections. Penetration testing can reveal weaknesses in your security infrastructure.

Data Classification: Categorize data into sensitivity levels and apply extra precautions to highly sensitive data, labeling it appropriately.

Data Retention Policies: Establish clear data retention policies, specifying how long data should be retained and when it should be securely disposed of, in compliance with relevant industry data retention regulations.

Data privacy and security are inherently linked to ethical considerations. Here are practical tips to make data ethics a guiding principle:

Transparency: Be transparent about data collection and usage to build trust with users who value knowing how their data is handled.

Consent: Seek informed consent from users before collecting their data and ensure that the process of opting in or out is straightforward.

Data Minimization: Collect only the data necessary for the intended purpose to reduce the volume of sensitive information.

Data Governance: Appoint a dedicated data protection officer or team, responsible for staying informed about data privacy laws and best practices.

Training and Awareness: Provide comprehensive training on data privacy and security for your team, fostering a culture of awareness as the primary defense against data breaches.

Incident Response Plan: Develop a well-structured plan to address data breaches, minimize potential damage, and demonstrate your unwavering commitment to data protection.

Building an AI/ML Team

In product management, constructing an effective AI/ML team parallels the formation of a highly capable product development unit, with each member playing a crucial role in the success of your product initiatives. In this section, we explore the vital functions of data scientists, engineers, and domain experts in our team and how their specific proficiency collectively shapes our product strategy.

Data Scientists: Strategic Thinkers

Think of data scientists as strategic thinkers in the product management context. They are primarily responsible for extracting valuable insights from data, which serve as the foundation for our product's features and functionalities. Their expertise lies in meticulously examining and refining data, uncovering hidden patterns, and translating these insights into actionable components that drive our product forward.

Data scientists also serve as the architects behind our data-driven product innovations, crafting complex machine learning models that underpin our product's capabilities. They closely collaborate with engineers to ensure that these models are not merely theoretical constructs but can be practically implemented to enhance user experience.

Moreover, data scientists are akin to the craftsmen of feature engineering, transforming raw data into the fundamental building blocks of our data-driven product.

Machine Learning Engineers: Implementation Specialists

In our product management realm, machine learning engineers are the implementers, responsible for translating our data-driven concepts into practical product features. They bridge the gap between data science and software engineering, converting our innovative ideas into tangible assets.

Machine learning engineers manage the intricate process of deploying data-driven models into our product, ensuring seamless and efficient functionality within real-world applications. They excel at optimizing these models for scalability and efficiency, much like engineers fine-tuning a product's performance to maximize user satisfaction.

Furthermore, they establish monitoring systems, acting as vigilant quality controllers to ensure the smooth operation of our product's data-driven features, and enabling real-time adjustments when necessary.

Domain Experts: Real-World Guides

Domain experts play the role of real-world guides in our product development journey, providing insight into how our product aligns with the unique needs and objectives of our users, based on their deep industry knowledge.

They also function as guardians of data quality, identifying anomalies that might escape the scrutiny of data scientists, thereby ensuring the reliability and trustworthiness of the data underpinning our product.

Furthermore, they act as evaluators, akin to the discerning critics of our product. Domain experts validate model outputs against industry-specific criteria, ensuring that our product's data-driven features meet the highest standards and fulfill the expectations of our target audience.

Case Exercise: Assembling Cross-functional Teams for Success.

In the evolving landscape of modern business, adapting to emerging technologies has become a key to maintaining competitiveness. This case study delves into a practical approach - the implementation of a cross-functional AI/ML team within our product management framework. Comprising data scientists, machine learning engineers, and domain experts, this team is envisioned to serve as a catalyst for product innovation, user experience enhancement, and the continued success of our product offerings.

Key Questions and Problem Statement:

1. Addressing Market Dynamics: Our first consideration is understanding how AI/ML adoption aligns with the ever-shifting dynamics of the market. How can these technologies enable us to adapt to the fast-changing landscape and evolving customer needs?

2. Assessing Our Resources: An essential step is to evaluate our current organizational capabilities in terms of AI/ML resources and expertise. By doing so, we can determine the gaps and limitations that hinder us from fully utilizing AI/ML effectively.

3. Identifying Challenges and Opportunities: This part explores the challenges and opportunities within our product management process. By identifying the pain points and recognizing areas for potential improvement, we can align our AI/ML initiatives with precise objectives.

Solution Overview:

Our proposed solution focuses on establishing a cross-functional AI/ML team. This team will be a blend of data scientists, machine learning engineers, and domain experts, united by their diverse skills. The collaborative synergy of these experts is poised to address our product management challenges and foster innovation.

Implementation Plan:

1. Team Formation: We will initiate the process by recruiting and onboarding professionals in the fields of data science, machine learning, and domain-specific expertise. This diversity will bolster the team's skill set.

2. Tool and Resource Allocation: A fundamental aspect of this initiative is the provision of essential tools, software, and data resources to empower the team for effective work.

3. Project Identification: To align with our product management goals and the needs of the market, we shall identify the initial AI/ML projects for implementation.

4. Project Execution: The cross-functional team will be tasked with the practical execution of the identified projects, nurturing a culture of collaboration and shared objectives.

5. Evaluation and Iteration: Continuous monitoring of project progress, outcome assessments, and the iterative adaptation of strategies will be the cornerstones of this initiative.

6. Documentation and Training: For sustained growth, we will establish a robust documentation process for AI/ML models and provide ongoing training opportunities to ensure that team members remain updated with evolving technologies.

Expected Benefits:

1. Improved Products: The incorporation of AI/ML will lead to product enhancements, resulting in improved user experiences

and customer satisfaction.

2. Data-Driven Decision-Making: The ability to make informed, data-driven decisions will lead to successful product launches and optimized resource allocation.

3. Competitive Advantage: The differentiating factor will set our products apart in the market, attracting new customers, and retaining our existing customer base.

Cost Estimate:

The practical implementation of the cross-functional AI/ML team will involve budget allocation for:

- Team Salaries: This includes recruitment and compensation for data scientists, machine learning engineers, and domain experts.
- Technology and Software: Investment in AI/ML tools, software, and infrastructure.
- Training and Development: A budget earmarked for continuous training and skill enhancement to keep the team updated with the ever-evolving AI/ML landscape.
- Project Resources: Funding is allocated for project-specific resources and data acquisition.

Conclusion:

The integration of AI/ML into our product management strategy is not only a forward-looking step but also an essential one. The establishment of a cross-functional AI/ML team not only enhances our product offerings but also fortifies our position in a market characterized by rapid change. This strategic investment in innovation will drive growth and significantly contribute to our long-term success.

End-to-end operations of AI/ML model

The world of AI and machine learning is filled with buzzwords and concepts like MLOps, ModelOps, DataOps, and GovernanceOps. It's essential to break down these terms and understand their fundamental importance in the AI/ML process.

AI/ML Operations: AI/ML Operations, collectively known as MLOps, streamline the development and deployment of AI models. Think of MLOps as your toolbox for managing models efficiently. They automate deployment, fine-tune models, monitor performance, and optimize resource allocation. MLOps take the guesswork out of AI deployment, making it quicker, cost-effective, and more reliable.

The Role of ModelOps: Model Operations, or ModelOps, zooms in on the model lifecycle. They provide structure for model development, automate deployment, and ensure ongoing efficiency. ModelOps simplifies experimentation, allowing data scientists to focus on model quality. It's all about maintaining reliability, streamlining model updates, and optimizing resources. Think of ModelOps as your model's best friend throughout its journey.

The Power of DataOps: Data Operations, or DataOps, forms the backbone of AI/ML by ensuring data quality and accessibility. Picture DataOps as the quality control department for your data. They guarantee reliable data, make it readily available for model development, and assist in data preprocessing. In essence, DataOps prepares your data for a successful AI/ML journey, providing a strong foundation for model development.

Governance and Ethical Considerations: Governance Operations, or GovernanceOps, focuses on ethical and governance aspects. They ensure that data and models comply with ethical and legal standards, thereby establishing trust and transparency. GovernanceOps guides the ethical use of AI/ML and ensures adherence to regulations. It's about aligning AI/ML practices with society's expectations and ensuring responsible AI deployment.

In summary, these concepts might sound complex, but their fundamental purpose is to make AI/ML more accessible, efficient, and responsible. They are the driving force behind streamlined operations, reliable models, quality data, and ethical AI/ML practices. By demystifying these terms, we make them more approachable for everyone involved in the AI/ML journey.

The enterprise's journey towards AI/ML excellence unfolds across multiple levels, as it progressively unveils the vast potential of artificial intelligence and machine learning. This journey is a series of distinct phases, each representing a pivotal milestone in the pursuit of AI/ML excellence.

AIM-PLUS

Phase 1: Acquaint with AI/ML (AIM)

In the initial phase, organizations take the first steps in understanding AI/ML. This stage is all about AIM:

- A: Awareness & Learning: Employees and leadership equip themselves with a fundamental understanding of AI/ML, promoting knowledge sharing. Platforms like Coursera, edX, and Udacity offer online courses and certifications in AI/ML, allowing employees to upskill.

- I: Initial Testing: Pilot projects are initiated, serving as initial testing grounds to gauge the practical application of AI/ML. Tools like Jupyter Notebook and Google Collab assist in creating and testing AI/ML PoCs before full-scale deployment.

- M: Multidisciplinary Team: A diverse, cross-functional team is assembled, incorporating the skills of data scientists, engineers, and domain experts. Tools like Slack and Microsoft Teams enable cross-functional teams to communicate and collaborate effectively on AI/ML projects.

Phase 2: Proving Effectiveness (PLUS)

The next phase is about proving the effectiveness of AI/ML. We label it PLUS:

- P: Pilot Expansion: Successful pilot projects are expanded to demonstrate that AI/ML can effectively solve real business problems. Data preparation platforms like Apache Nifi help clean, preprocess, and organize data.

- L: Lean Data Management: Data is prepared, organized, and made accessible, following DataOps principles without unnecessary complexity. Observability tools are used to monitor the metadata and lineage.

- U: Use Automation: Automation is introduced into model development and deployment, streamlining processes. Tools like TensorFlow, PyTorch, and Scikit-learn are widely used for building and deploying AI/ML models.

- S: Scale-Up Operations: MLOps, including monitoring, deployment, and optimization, are fundamental to scaling AI/ML operations. Tools like MLflow, Kubeflow, and Seldon facilitate model management, monitoring, and deployment automation.

Phase 3: Ethical & Regulatory Adherence (ERA)

As AI/ML becomes an integral part of the business, ethical and regulatory considerations are essential. We abbreviate this as ERA:

- E: Ethical Guidelines: The organization establishes ethical guidelines to ensure AI/ML is used responsibly and ethically. AI ethics assessment tools like EthicalOS and Ethical AI Guidelines, help ensure responsible AI use.

- R: Regulations Compliance: Compliance with industry-specific rules and regulations is a priority, aligning with legal standards. Platforms like OneTrust and TrustArc assist in managing and demonstrating compliance with data privacy regulations.

- A: Assure Transparency: Ensuring transparency in AI/ML operations is crucial to maintain trust and accountability. Tools like IBM AI OpenScale and Lime provide transparency and explainability in AI/ML models.

Phase 4: Continuous Enhancement (CEC)

AI/ML isn't stagnant; it's a continuous process. We call this phase CEC:

- C: Continuous Model Management: Models are managed and updated continually, staying current and reliable. AI/ML model management platforms such as Apache Airflow, Metaflow and Prometheus help with model versioning, monitoring, and updating.

- E: Embrace Feedback: Feedback mechanisms are integrated to gather user input and continuously refine models. Feedback collection tools like SurveyMonkey and UserVoice gather user feedback for model improvement.

- C: Cost-Effective AI/ML: Managing costs efficiently is a central focus, optimizing resources for maximum value. General Cost management tools help optimize AI/ML operational costs.

Phase 5: Cultural Integration & Growth (CIG)

In this final phase, AI/ML becomes ingrained in the organization's culture. We refer to this as CIG:

- C: Cultural Transformation: The organization fosters a culture of AI/ML innovation, where employees are encouraged to propose solutions and think creatively. Innovation management tools like IdeaScale and Spigit facilitate idea generation and innovation culture.

- I: Ingrain Data-Driven Strategies: AI/ML becomes the cornerstone of strategic decisions, optimizing resources and enhancing customer experiences. Business intelligence tools such as Tableau, Superset and Power BI enable data-driven decision-making across the organization.

- G: Growth & Learning: Continuous learning and development opportunities are provided to employees to stay at the forefront of AI/ML technology. Learning management systems (LMS) like Moodle and TalentLMS support employee training and development in AI/ML.

AI/ML Readiness Assessment Template for Executives

Phase 1: Acquaint with AI/ML (AIM)

1. Awareness & Learning:
   - No awareness (0 marks)
   - Limited understanding (1 mark)
   - Basic awareness (2 marks)
   - Thorough understanding (3 marks)

2. Initial Testing:
   - No pilot projects (0 marks)
   - Small-scale tests (1 mark)
   - Some pilot projects (2 marks)
   - Multiple successful pilots (3 marks)

3. Multidisciplinary Team:
   - No cross-functional team (0 marks)
   - Team with a single skill set (1 mark)
   - Limited cross-functional team (2 marks)
   - Diverse, balanced team (3 marks)

Phase 2: Proving Effectiveness (PLUS)

4. Pilot Expansion:
   - No expansion (0 marks)
   - Limited scaling (1 mark)
   - Moderate expansion (2 marks)
   - Successful scale-up (3 marks)

5. Lean Data Management:
   - Data not organized (0 marks)
   - Basic data organization (1 mark)
   - Effective data organization (2 marks)
   - DataOps principles applied (3 marks)

6. Use Automation:
   - No automation (0 marks)
   - Minimal automation (1 mark)
   - Some automation (2 marks)
   - Significant automation (3 marks)

7. Scale-Up Operations:
   * Limited monitoring (0 marks)
   * Basic monitoring (1 mark)
   * Active monitoring (2 marks)
   * Comprehensive MLOps (3 marks)

Phase 3: Ethical & Regulatory Adherence (ERA)

8. Ethical Guidelines:
   * No ethical guidelines (0 marks)
   * Initial guidelines (1 mark)
   * Established guidelines (2 marks)
   * Comprehensive ethical framework (3 marks)

9. Regulation Compliance:
   * Non-compliance (0 marks)
   * Partial compliance (1 mark)
   * Basic compliance (2 marks)
   * Full compliance (3 marks)

10. Assure Transparency:
   * Limited transparency (0 marks)
   * Some transparency (1 mark)
   * Transparent practices (2 marks)
   * Full transparency (3 marks)

Phase 4: Continuous Enhancement (CEC)

11. Continuous Model Management:
   * No framework (0 marks)
   * Basic framework (1 mark)
   * Ongoing management (2 marks)
   * Comprehensive model lifecycle management (3 marks)

12. Embrace Feedback:
   * No feedback collection (0 marks)
   * Limited feedback (1 mark)
   * Incorporating feedback (2 marks)
   * Proactive feedback integration (3 marks)

13. Cost-Effective AI/ML:
- Cost inefficiency (0 marks)
- Cost awareness (1 mark)
- Cost optimization (2 marks)
- Efficient resource allocation (3 marks)

Phase 5: Cultural Integration & Growth (CIG)

14. Cultural Transformation:
- No culture change (0 marks)
- Some innovation encouragement (1 mark)
- Encouraging innovation (2 marks)
- Innovation culture (3 marks)

15. Ingrain Data-Driven Strategies:
- Limited integration (0 marks)
- Partial integration (1 mark)
- Strategic integration (2 marks)
- Central to decisions (3 marks)

16. Growth & Learning:
- Limited learning opportunities (0 marks)
- Basic learning initiatives (1 mark)
- Learning programs (2 marks)
- Comprehensive learning (3 marks)

Total Marks (Sum of checked options):

- 0 to 15 marks: Early Stage
- 16 to 30 marks: Intermediate Stage
- 31 to 45 marks: Advanced Stage
- 46 to 60 marks: Mature Stage

This template allows executives to assess their organization's AI/ML readiness by selecting options and calculating the total marks to determine the current state of readiness.

Regulatory Compliance

The complexity of regulations and guidelines can pose challenges, but it's essential to ensure not only the successful implementation of AI/ML but also the protection of data privacy, security, and ethical use. In this section, we'll delve into two significant pillars of AI/ML compliance: GDPR and HIPAA, as well as the importance of adhering to industry-specific guidelines.

GDPR: Safeguarding Data Privacy

The General Data Protection Regulation (GDPR) is a pivotal piece of legislation that extends its reach far beyond the European Union (EU). It sets rigorous standards for the processing of personal data, which is particularly relevant when it comes to data used in AI/ML algorithms. Organizations must adhere to key principles, including data minimization, transparency, data portability, the right to explanation, and consent management. These principles affect how AI/ML systems collect, process, and utilize data, emphasizing the need for clarity, user consent, and responsible data handling.

HIPAA: Protecting Healthcare Data

Healthcare organizations must uphold the standards of the Health Insurance Portability and Accountability Act (HIPAA) when dealing with patient data in the context of AI/ML. HIPAA compliance is especially vital to safeguard patient privacy and security. Key considerations include data encryption, access control, audit trails, and data anonymization. These measures are critical in ensuring that AI/ML-driven processes maintain the integrity and confidentiality of patient information, while still harnessing the benefits of AI in healthcare.

Industry-Specific Guidelines

Various industries have their own sets of guidelines and standards concerning AI/ML compliance. For example, the financial sector adheres to regulations like the Basel Committee's "Principles for the Sound Management of Operational Risk" to ensure AI/ML aligns with risk assessment requirements. Similarly, the automotive industry follows standards such as ISO 21448 to guarantee safety in autonomous vehicles. Compliance with these industry-specific guidelines is pivotal to maintaining regulatory standards while harnessing AI/ML's innovation and competitive potential, as it requires a deep understanding of the unique demands of each industry.

Case Study: Comflix - Transforming Content Recommendation using AI/ML

Comflix, the global streaming giant, has become synonymous with content personalization through the power of AI and machine learning. Their journey to perfecting content recommendation algorithms, using tools like Metaflow, provides invaluable insights into the world of AI/ML product management.

Challenge: In the early 2000s, Comflix faced a substantial challenge. They aimed to deliver personalized content recommendations to enhance user experience. Without efficient recommendations, users might not discover the vast catalog of shows and movies, which could lead to customer churn.

The AI/ML Solution: Comflix leveraged AI and machine learning algorithms to create a recommendation engine. They organized the Comflix Prize, a competition with a million-dollar prize for the team that could improve the recommendation algorithm's accuracy by 10%. This challenge has attracted data scientists and AI experts worldwide, resulting in innovative approaches. Comflix employed tools like Metaflow to streamline the development and deployment of their machine learning workflows. Metaflow helped the teams maintain reproducibility, scalability, and a more organized approach to machine learning pipelines.

Success Metrics:

- Improved User Retention: Implementation of AI-powered recommendations significantly increased user retention and engagement. It led to customers discovering new content, making them more likely to renew their subscriptions.

- Reduced Churn: The personalized content recommendations reduced customer churn rates, leading to substantial cost savings in customer acquisition.

- Increased Viewer Satisfaction: Users reported higher satisfaction with Comflix, as they found content that was more aligned with their preferences, reducing the time spent searching for something to watch.

Lessons Learned:

1. Data is Paramount: Comflix realized that high-quality, diverse data is the lifeblood of any AI/ML system. They collected data on user behavior, preferences, and content attributes to train and fine-tune their recommendation models. Tools like Metaflow helped manage the data pipeline efficiently.

2. Iterate and Experiment: Comflix understood that AI/ML systems are not static. They continually refined their recommendation algorithms through experimentation and A/B testing to optimize user satisfaction, using Metaflow to maintain workflow consistency.

3. User-Centric Design: Focusing on delivering personalized experiences based on individual user behavior and preferences is key. Comflix tailored their recommendations to meet each user's unique tastes.

4. Interdisciplinary Teams: Cross-functional teams involving data scientists, engineers, and domain experts collaborated to create a recommendation system that aligned with both user preferences and business goals.

5. Scalability Matters: As Comflix expanded globally, they ensured that their recommendation system could scale with the growing user base and content library. This scalability was vital to maintaining high-quality recommendations.

6. Continued Innovation: Comflix continues to innovate in AI/ML. They have incorporated deep learning models, reinforcement learning, and natural language processing to further improve content recommendations and enhance content

creation. These innovations have solidified Comflix as a frontrunner in the streaming industry.

The Comflix case study exemplifies how AI/ML and workflow management tools can revolutionize product management. This leads to enhanced user experiences, increased retention, and tangible business growth, all while maintaining data quality and workflow efficiency. It serves as a testament to the importance of data, user-centric design, and continuous innovation in the realm of AI/ML product management.

Case Study: Kuber - Transforming Transportation with AI/ML

Kuber, the global ride-hailing giant, has revolutionized the transportation industry through the innovative application of AI and machine learning. This case study explores Kuber's journey in implementing AI/ML, shaping the future of transportation, and offering valuable insights into the realm of AI/ML product management.

Challenge: Kuber's mission to make transportation as reliable as running water presented a significant challenge - efficiently matching riders with drivers while minimizing wait times and prices. Meeting this challenge required real-time data analysis, dynamic pricing, and route optimization.

The AI/ML Solution: Kuber employed AI and machine learning to build a recommendation system that connects riders with drivers. Here's how AI/ML played a pivotal role:

- Demand Forecasting: Kuber developed algorithms to predict rider demand patterns in specific areas, allowing them to pre-position drivers for anticipated ride requests.

- Dynamic Pricing: Machine learning models adjust pricing in real-time, factoring in demand, weather, and traffic, and optimizing the balance between rider affordability and driver income.

- Routing and Navigation: Kuber used AI to optimize routes, considering factors like traffic conditions and rider/driver locations, ensuring faster, more efficient trips.

Success Metrics:

- Efficiency: The AI/ML system improved driver utilization and reduced passenger wait times, leading to increased efficiency in the transportation network.

- Customer Satisfaction: Enhanced routing and dynamic pricing led to improved user satisfaction as riders experienced shorter wait times and more affordable fares.

- Driver Earnings: Drivers benefitted from increased ride requests and optimized routes, leading to higher earnings and job satisfaction.

Lessons Learned:

1. Data-Driven Decision-Making: Kuber's success depends on real-time data analysis. They collected and analyzed vast amounts of data to make informed decisions regarding demand forecasting, pricing, and routing.

2. Dynamic Pricing Sensitivity: Kuber learned that striking the right balance between pricing and rider/driver incentives is critical. This requires ongoing testing and experimentation with pricing algorithms.

3. User Experience Matters: User experience is at the heart of AI/ML product management. Kuber continually refined their app and algorithms to make the experience seamless for both riders and drivers.

4. Safety and Compliance: Safety and compliance remained the top priorities for Kuber, and AI/ML played a role in verifying driver identities and optimizing safety features.

5. Data Security and Privacy: Handling vast amounts of user data comes with significant responsibilities. Kuber needed to prioritize data security and user privacy while benefiting from

data-driven insights.

Continued Innovation: Kuber continues to innovate in the AI/ML space. They are exploring self-driving cars and further optimizing their transportation network to reduce emissions and improve sustainability. They use AI/ML not only for ride-hailing but also for their food delivery service, Kuber Eats.

The Kuber case study demonstrate how AI and machine learning can transform traditional industries. By focusing on data-driven decisions, user experience, and ongoing innovation, Kuber has disrupted the transportation sector, setting a benchmark for AI/ML product management.

AI -First

In the business landscape, AI-first companies have made a mark with their innovations. These innovators have embraced the power of artificial intelligence and machine learning (AI/ML) to achieve remarkable milestones, distinguishing themselves from corporations and traditional businesses that are yet to fully adopt AI/ML into their daily operations.

Transforming Industries: AI-First companies are rewriting the rules in their respective industries. In healthcare, for example, predictive analytics are used to improve patient care and reduce medical errors. In finance, they leverage AI/ML for algorithmic trading, risk assessment, and fraud detection, putting themselves ahead in the financial sector. They haven't merely integrated AI/ML into their workflows; they've made it a central part of their operations.

Competitive Edge: The competitive advantage of AI-First companies arises from their ability to turn data into insights. They understand that AI/ML is not just a tool but a catalyst for proactive decision-making. While traditional corporations and legacy businesses may still rely on manual data analysis, AI-First companies can quickly identify emerging trends, customer preferences, and potential bottlenecks. This agility gives them a strategic edge that sets them apart in the marketplace.

Customer-Focused Innovation: AI-First companies have also

mastered customer-centric innovation. They use AI/ML to customize products and services based on individual preferences, that enhance customer satisfaction and loyalty. In contrast, companies lagging in AI/ML integration often struggle with generic, one-size-fits-all offerings that cannot keep up with the evolving market demands.

Foresight and Adaptability: AI-First companies demonstrate unique foresight and adaptability. They continuously refine their operations, looking for opportunities to automate tasks, reduce costs, and improve productivity. In doing so, they build a flexible and future-ready infrastructure, while many of their counterparts' grapple with legacy systems and manual processes that hinder growth and efficiency.

The Gap Widens: As AI-First companies continue to excel, the gap between them and corporations or legacy businesses that resist AI/ML integration grows wider. The latter often wrestle with inefficiencies, operational challenges, and an inability to unlock the full potential of their data. The pace of AI/ML innovation doesn't wait for anyone, and the divide may only become more significant over time.

In this chapter, which focuses on AI Product Management within the AI/ML landscape, we've delved into the dynamic world of artificial intelligence and machine learning and their essential role in product management. Throughout the chapter, we've explored critical facets such as identifying AI/ML opportunities, crafting effective product strategies, managing data, building cross-functional teams, and comprehending the complete AI/ML model operations. Additionally, we've introduced the AIM-PLUS framework as a practical tool and offered an AI/ML readiness assessment template tailored for executives. To emphasize the significance of AI/ML integration, we've also underscored the competitive edge enjoyed by AI-First companies over those who have yet to embrace these technologies. Armed with these insights and practical resources, you're well-prepared to navigate the ever-evolving landscape of AI/ML product management and foster innovation in our dynamic technological era.

10 AUTHOR NOTE

As we conclude our in-depth exploration of the dynamic field of product management, we hope that this book will serve as an invaluable resource for your pursuit of excellence in this ever-evolving discipline. From core principles to AI/ML integration, this book covers a broad spectrum of strategies, tactics, and insights to empower you in your role as a product manager.

Product management demands a blend of intuition and data-driven decision-making. This book provides a comprehensive guide that encompasses the essential concepts, techniques, and approaches necessary for success in this multifaceted role.

Throughout these pages, we've delved into key areas:

Understanding the essence of product management and its pivotal role in today's technology-driven world. We've explored the significance of platform products and the specific challenges they present to product managers. Craft a compelling product strategy, shape your vision and comprehend the competitive landscape. The pivotal role of customers in shaping your product, including conducting customer interviews, and creating user stories. Prioritization methodologies for efficient resource allocation. Execution strategies, such as product release, road-mapping, and post-launch monitoring. The importance of effective communication with stakeholders and cross-functional teams, and handling challenging conversations. We've also discussed the importance of documentation and the advantages it provides in terms of clarity and accountability. Building high-performing teams and fostering an environment of inclusion, motivation, and continuous development. Cultivating a culture of innovation, embracing experimentation, and leveraging innovative frameworks. Addressing the emerging challenges of AI/ML in product management, from identifying opportunities to end-to-end operations.

As a product manager, you play a pivotal role in driving transformative change. Your role is not solely about creating products; it's about crafting experiences, solving problems, and leading your organization toward success.

In conclusion, always strive to:

- Maintain a customer-centric approach by actively listening, understanding, and adapting to their needs.
- Foster a collaborative environment that embraces diversity, innovation, and cross-functional teamwork.
- Embrace experimentation and remain open to learning from both successes and failures.
- Be a continuous learner, adapting to new technologies and trends, such as AI and ML.
- Prioritize effective communication, documentation, and leadership, as these are the keys to success.

We trust that this book has provided you with the knowledge, tools, and inspiration you need to become an outstanding product manager. Remember that your path doesn't stop here; it unfolds with each new challenge and each fresh opportunity.

Thank you for joining us on this insightful journey. May your mission in the dynamic field of product management be filled with innovation, growth, and meaningful impact.

We Wish you the very best in your product management endeavors.

ABOUT THE AUTHOR

Abhishek Agarwal is an accomplished and award-winning product manager, known for his outstanding career with influential leadership positions at Fortune 500 giants including Unilever, Amazon, and Hewlett Packard Enterprise (HPE). His exceptional achievements are evident in his ability to streamline AI/ML model development, making open-source frameworks more accessible for data scientists and demonstrating his remarkable talent for driving innovation in the fields of Artificial Intelligence and Machine Learning.

Abhishek's educational journey is equally impressive, encompassing renowned institutions like Yale University and the Indian Institute of Technology (IIT). This academic background has shaped a distinctive combination of academic excellence and practical expertise, setting him apart as a distinguished professional in his field.

His remarkable thought leadership and invaluable insights have earned him recognition in leading media outlets, underlining the significant impact he has had on the constantly evolving landscape of technology and innovation. Abhishek Agarwal's contributions have been celebrated and awarded, solidifying his position as a distinguished leader in the industry.

A

A/B Testing · 156, 157, 162
acceptance criteria · 26
Additional Reading · 34
Agile · 27, 67, 68, 71, 83, 84, 85, 86, 149, 150, 151, 162
AI -First · 191
AI/ML · v, 164, 165, 166, 167, 168, 169, 170, 171, 172, 173, 174, 176, 177, 178, 179, 180, 181, 182, 183, 185, 186, 187, 188, 189, 190, 191, 192, 193, 194, 195
AIM-PLUS · v, 180, 192
API · 113, 115
Artificial Intelligence · 165, 195

B

Behavioral Questions · 130, 131
Beta Testing · 87, 90, 91, 92, 93, 95
Blue Ocean · 13, 14, 15
Business Case · 93

C

Case Studies · 138
CEO · 1, 2
Continuous Enhancement · 181, 184
Customer Interviews · 22
Customer Support · 76, 98, 123

D

Data Acquisition · 172
Data Analysis · 157
Data Privacy · 173, 186
Data Scientists · 174
Data Security · 96, 99, 190
Debrief · 149, 151, 152, 154
Documentation · 112, 113, 114, 115, 134, 177
Domain Experts · 175

E

Empowering · 141
Engineers · 104, 175
Ethical Considerations · 179
Example · 11, 31, 32, 71
Exercise · 5, 105, 109, 148, 150, 151, 153, 156, 176
Experimentation · 161, 162

F

Feedback · 41, 78, 89, 91, 92, 94, 99, 107, 111, 121, 123, 137, 138, 139, 142, 145, 146, 157, 169, 182, 184
Feedback Loops · 89, 99, 123, 146
Framework · 64

G

Gamification · 138
GDPR · 186
GenAI · 165
Governance · 174, 179

H

HIPAA · 186
Hiring · 31, 32, 126
Hypothesis Testing · 156

I

Ideate · 149
Impact versus Effort Analysis · 43
Incentive · 136
Interviews · 128, 129, 132, 133

J

JTBD · 28, 29, 30, 31, 32, 33, 42

K

Kano Model · 42, 49, 51, 52, 53, 64
Knowledge · 30, 116, 162, 165
KPIs · 23, 33, 77, 82, 97, 145, 156

L

Leader · 123

Lean Startup · 155, 156, 157, 158

M

Machine Learning · 165, 175, 195
mechanisms · 78, 91, 162, 182
Mobile App · 160
MoSCoW Method · 42
MVP · 46, 93, 155, 156, 157, 158

O

Onboarding · 126, 134, 135, 141, 160
OP1/OP2 · 20
Outbound Product Management · 5
Outcomes-based approach · 32
Ownership · 76, 77, 141

P

Pivot · 155, 158
platform · 3, 4, 10, 12, 47, 71, 79, 80, 102, 104, 105, 131, 132, 139, 146, 193
Presentation · 149, 151, 152, 154, 158
Pricing · 15, 92, 189, 190
Prioritization · 27, 30, 39, 40, 41, 42, 51, 53, 58, 66, 109, 193
Prototype · 149, 154

R

Recruitment · 127, 141

Red Ocean · 13, 14, 15
Reflect · 37, 149, 151
Regulations Compliance · 181
Reporting · 99
RICE Framework · 42, 56, 58, 65
Role-Playing · 137

S

Sprint · 84, 150, 151
Stand-up · 84, 150
Success Metrics · 187, 190

T

Team · 76, 78, 83, 85, 112, 118, 119, 120, 122, 124, 126, 127, 134, 141, 142, 143, 145, 150, 174, 177, 178, 180, 183
Template · 18, 182
Test · 149, 160

U

user stories · 66
User Stories · 25, 28, 48, 51, 58, 61
User testing · 152, 154

V

Value vs. Complexity Matrix · 42, 53, 54, 55, 56, 65
Vision and Mission · 8

W

WBR Format · 81
Weighted Scoring · 43, 59, 61, 66
Wireframing · 154
Workshops · 123, 138, 146
Workspace · 106, 107, 108, 110, 111, 112